Wooden Spoon

Rugby's charity supporting disadvantaged children and young people

WOODEN SPOON
RUGBYWORLD'07

Editor
Ian Robertson

Photographs
Getty Images

Queen Anne Press

A QUEEN ANNE PRESS BOOK

© Lennard Associates Limited 2006

First published in 2006 by
Queen Anne Press, a division of
Lennard Associates Limited
Mackerye End
Harpenden, Herts AL5 5DR

A catalogue entry is available from the British Library

ISBN 1 85291 668 0

Production Editor: Chris Marshall
Cover Design/Design Consultant: Paul Cooper
Printed and bound in Slovenia

The publishers would like to thank Getty Images for providing most of the photographs for this book.

The publishers would also like to thank Fotosport UK, Inphopics, Chris Thau and Wooden Spoon for additional material.

A la recherche du temps perdu

Contents

'Fan'atical

There's nothing ordinary about our support for Rugby Union

Positive Energy

FOREWORD

by HRH THE PRINCESS ROYAL

BUCKINGHAM PALACE

HRH The Princess Royal, Royal Patron of Wooden Spoon, opens the Wooden Spoon Arena at the Calvert Trust – Exmoor's Activity Centre for the Disabled in Devon.

Like a successful rugby side, Wooden Spoon's growth is built on good teamwork. A small staff team supports an impressive body of volunteers that organise nearly 150 fundraising events each year. The money raised at each of these events is doubled by Spoon's central fundraising effort. The volunteers, under the guidance of Spoon's Trustees, then have twice the funds available to invest in their local communities. In the past year, 71 new projects have been approved by the Trustees to benefit disadvantaged children and young people.

Children and young people requiring specialist health care have benefited, for example, from support towards phase two of the first children's hospital in Wales; the development of a teenage cancer website; adolescent care facilities and the purchase and training of a horse to give disabled children the chance to ride.

Spoon is passionate about education too. New libraries have been built, training centres opened and Special Needs schools supported. In rugby, Spoon worked closely with the Premiership sides to develop education and training schemes in socially deprived areas. Over 6,000 children have benefited in the first year. Other sports are taking note and Spoon is already working closely with several rugby league sides and their supporters.

The year produced a record number of projects. As Patron of Wooden Spoon, I invite you to lend your support to the charity, so that as a team we can achieve far more.

Anne

Wooden Spoon

Rugby's charity supporting disadvantaged children and young people

Ian Robertson: A Man of Many Words
by TRACEY LARCOMBE

Royal Patron: HRH The Princess Royal
Patrons: Rugby Football Union • Scottish Rugby Union
                 Welsh Rugby Union • Irish Rugby Football Union

As you might gather by the stories from those kind enough to respond to my requests for anecdotes on Ian Robertson for this feature, there are two words that spring to mind most frequently: betting and charm. As far as betting goes, Robbo can't really argue; almost everyone you talk to about the man has had a bet with him on something or other. Where charm is concerned, however, I am surprised to note he is rather less pleased and even a little put-out by this observation, preferring instead the word 'enthusiasm' to describe this particular character trait. But as one who has been on the receiving end of his 'enthusiasm' on more than one occasion, I am inclined to disagree. Let's face it, if anyone else opened a phone conversation with the words 'Is that Tracey big bum?' they would understandably get an earful; he somehow, with that soft Scottish lilt and gravelly chuckle, gets away with it.

'I admit I am a bit of a smoothie when I'm trying to get money out of people whether it's for Wooden Spoon or for Alastair Hignell's charity, I just go about it as a target. It's always better to be

nice than not; I'm friendly but it's nothing to do with charm.'

Whatever you say, Robbo. What he can't deny is that in the 20-odd years he has worked tirelessly for Spoon, he has managed to 'enthuse' hundreds of people into parting with thousands of pounds for the charity.

'I first got involved with Spoon in the late eighties through the former chief executive, David Roberts; he asked if I would speak at a series of events called the Thames Valley Luncheons. So I turned up and spoke at one, then another and another and I just thought it was a fantastic charity. The fact it was rugby-based was part of the beauty of it, the other part was the cause, the disadvantaged and disabled children. I just love it, it's incredibly well known and all the rugby players get involved and help out, which is wonderful.'

I'd hazard a guess you'd be hard-pressed to find someone more devoted to rugby and everything that surrounds it than Ian Robertson – from his early playing days as a wily fly half bartering with his No. 8 to make all his tackles for him so he could concentrate on being 'a flash harry' and making breaks to get the threequarter line going, to playing under the pseudonym Ian McPherson for Aberdeenshire when he was given an 'education or rugby' ultimatum by his professors, to the 22-hour marathon bus journey to attend an interview at Cambridge University.

Having proved his rugby prowess by snatching a ball hurled at him as he went through the professor's door and drop-kicking it into the waste-paper bin, Robertson played and won his blue for Cambridge. He then trialled for Scotland and a couple of months later got his first cap at Murrayfield against England. In the meantime he started teaching at Fettes College where Tony Blair was one of his pupils.

'Blair was incredibly bright but non-sporty, so I love seeing him now running around in tennis kit or playing football, because my memory of him was that he always had athlete's foot or a verruca. He certainly never turned up with any regularity on the rugby pitch, so we didn't have very much in common. But I did keep essays of around ten of the boys I really thought were very promising and his was one of the ones I kept.'

Four years and eight caps later, Robbo was 24 years old and ready to captain his country for the first time, when his rugby career came to an abrupt end. A bad tackle ripped his medial and cruciate ligaments, which in the early 1970s was a career-ending injury. He was told he would never play again. 'I was so disappointed; nothing quite beats playing and being in a team, but commentating comes a close second and you can do one a little longer than the other. It came about when I got a

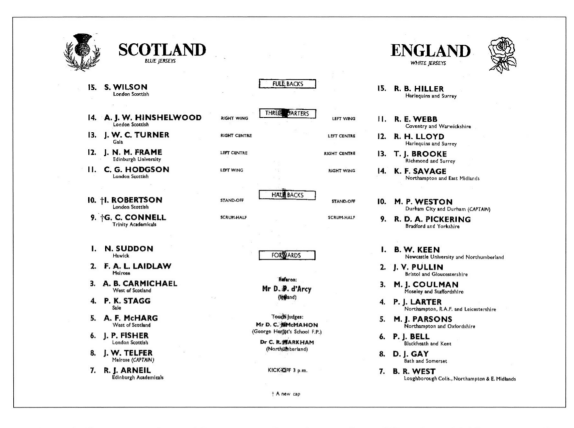

call from Cliff Morgan, who said he was switching from radio to TV and would I be interested in joining BBC Sport. So I came down [on the train this time!], met up with the boss, Angus MacKay, and started off as their expert summariser then started commentating. Only on Scotland and club games to begin with; they didn't let me anywhere near England for some reason.'

After 34 years spent on various halfway lines across the globe, he is still like an excitable Labrador puppy when it comes to talking about the game, and is modesty personified when it comes to dishing out compliments to those who have helped him along the way.

'I was very lucky because Bill McLaren and I were very good friends and I learnt everything he did, not just about rugby commentating but about broadcasting and it stood me in great stead. I was also very lucky to have known Cliff Morgan too, so the combination of the great preparation and everything that Bill did and the flair and charisma of Cliff Morgan were a great inspiration. I've got a route map and it's something that's governed my whole life; I was just very, very lucky I met two totally remarkable people who were at the peak of their powers, and like some sort of leech I sucked all the information I could from them.'

Robbo's work has obviously taken him to some of the biggest and most memorable sporting events in history; needless to say, a few have lodged in the memory banks as particularly special occasions. 'There have been some huge moments of broadcasting history for me: the Lions tours of '74, '89 and '97; Scotland's Grand Slam in '84; and the Calcutta Cups in '90, '94 and 2000.

'But probably my best life experience was when, after eight years of sporting isolation because of apartheid, South Africa were allowed back in and in the summer of '92 I flew out to cover their first international

Shortening the Odds – John Inverdale

'On the morning of the 2000 Guineas at Newmarket about six years ago, Robbo knew he just couldn't lose, and after the race he was strutting round telling anyone who would listen that he had confidently backed the winner. Of course, what he didn't say was that he had spent the last three months and ridiculous amounts of cash backing every single horse in the race, at some crazy odds, so every base was covered. I've no idea now how much he won but I doubt it was anywhere near what he spent in the process.'

Journalist? Me? – David Hands

'It was Ian's proud boast – it may still be – that he described his occupation in his passport as "travel agent" rather than journalist. Hence when the English press corps flew into Fiji in 1988 in the wake of a political coup in the islands, Ian was the only one of us allowed through customs. Journalists were not flavour of the month at that time, there having been a number of critical reports in Australian newspapers of the architects of the coup, but we were not disposed to argue with the large gun-bearing soldiers on duty at Suva airport.

So the England team flew on to Nadi to prepare for the international with Fiji and we loitered behind, wondering whether we would have to pick up the result from local agencies, until the barriers to our entry were raised and, late in the evening – hot but relieved – we passed through customs. Ian met us on the other side; it was, he declared, only his intervention with higher authorities that had eased our way. At that stage, whatever the truth of the matter, we were happy to believe him and all journalistic grains of salt were suspended.'

BELOW Ian Robertson (second from right) on duty at fly half for Scotland during their memorable 6-3 victory over South Africa at Murrayfield in 1969.

FACING PAGE The line-ups on the occasion of Ian Robertson's international debut for Scotland, against England at Murrayfield in 1968.

rugby game at Ellis Park against New Zealand. F.W. de Klerk and Nelson Mandela were there, and although all the journalists were told there would be no interviews, I was the only one who got in by bluffing my way past the guards in the banqueting area with a tape recorder under my jacket. I got an interview with Mr Mandela and had a chat, then I met him again two years later and he remembered meeting me. It was just a moment, a person and an occasion that would stand out above all else forever.'

Another stand-out occasion was of course the 2003 World Cup, from which Robbo's commentary on Johnny's winning dropped-goal has gone down in the annals of rugby history. But when it comes to defending their title in 2007, on current form England may struggle.

'It just went unbelievably well in 2003; they had such a phenomenal team there that my granny could probably have coached them to win it. This time around, it's extremely unlikely England will flop completely because they have such a reservoir of players. They won't be favourites to win but they will cruise through their pool without the slightest problem. I would certainly expect England to get through to the semi-finals without having to be a really, really good team.

'They've had three very bad seasons so they've got to rebuild, but they've got massive resources so it's not going to be that difficult to cobble a team together to make a thoroughly decent fist of it in the Six Nations. I would be surprised if England weren't in the top half of the table this season; that would be a major shock. One of the main reasons for the disappointments of the last two years in particular has been selection; that's been shocking and also the *use* of resources has been bad. But I'm sure England will bounce back.'

If only we could all share his optimism, which is another word that crops up often where Robertson is concerned; if a personality can be infectious, it is impossible for his energy and buoyancy not to rub off onto anyone in the vicinity.

Don't Spend it all at Once! – Damian Hopley

'I had a wager with Robbo in the run-up to the ill-fated 2005 British & Irish Lions tour to New Zealand that Neil Back would play in at least one of the Tests over the summer. In front of a well-heeled crowd of rugby dignitaries Robbo accepted my £200 bet, and immediately began to brag about this being the easiest money he had made since Scotland had beaten England in *that* game back in 1990.

'Not unsurprisingly for Robbo, he came unstuck when Backy played in the first Test, and I immediately sent him a good luck text informing him that 4 x £50 notes would suffice. In true tartan fashion, I didn't hear a peep from him for six (!) months, and it was only when I realised we were attending a dinner to help those poor underprivileged children from my alma mater, Harrow School, that I seized the opportunity to confront him.

'Stuttering like a child on his first day at school, Robbo offered a compromise whereby he would pay me £100 there and then, as long as I agreed to take him to lunch at an appropriate hostelry, where he would give me the remaining £100. Nearing the end of my tether, I reluctantly accepted and, beaming like a village idiot, the voice of BBC rugby pulled from his bag two commemorative Scottish £50 notes encased in unbreakable, bulletproof glass that were issued to commemorate the opening of the splendid new RBS HQ at Gogaburn outside Edinburgh. I should have known better than to expect a straightforward settlement from Robbo. Bet in haste, repent at leisure – you have been warned!'

Follow that Bus! – Alastair Hignell

'There are many instances of Robbo's infamous charm being put to full effect, but my particular favourite was when we were once terribly lost in Scotland whilst looking for the international team training camp in Livingston. I was driving and Robbo was navigating ... after a while he got out to ask directions at a bus queue. So there we were, busy trying to get out of our predicament, when the bus driver pulled up and instantly recognised Robbo. Without a second thought, he loaded up his passengers and then insisted we follow him as he drove us to Scotland's training ground, completely deviating from his bus route!'

FACING PAGE Ian Robertson in familiar guise as auctioneer at a Scottish Spoon function.

BELOW With the BBC team that covered the 2005 British & Irish Lions tour of New Zealand. From left to right: Robbo, Jason Leonard, David Elliott (MD Greene King Pub Partners), Jill Douglas, Alastair Hignell, Eric Peters.

'I'm a very optimistic person; every time I go anywhere I expect it to be brilliant. As far as work goes I can go off to watch Worcester against Bath and expect to see one of the greatest games of rugby ever, so I do get disappointed every so often. I love my job and I carry the same philosophy in life; the cup is always half-full not half-empty. I like to spread glad tidings; even when things go wrong I try not to mope around and complain. I just enjoy everything I do.'

I must say when our interview comes to an end after a superb dinner and such lively conversation, it is with real regret I have to leave. Aside, of course, from his closing remark as I self-consciously walk away to get my cab: 'See you again soon big bum!' Grrrrrr ...

Postscript from Geoff Morris, Chief Executive of Wooden Spoon:

Scarcely a day goes by without Ian's name cropping up in conversation, indeed it is part of the Wooden Spoon vernacular! Letters arrive in the morning post with scribbled notes and enclosed cheques. The notes say something like: 'Mr Robertson spoke at our annual dinner last week and persuaded us to make a donation to Wooden Spoon.' Notes from Ian himself are usually not so straightforward: 'Geoff, last year I had a bet with six people in the audience that Scotland would score more points than....and for each point either way an extra £1 would be given to Wooden Spoon. Here's a cheque for £241, didn't I do well?'

For several years, Ian has consistently raised more money for Spoon than any other single person. Editing *Wooden Spoon Rugby World* is just one of the many ways Ian helps us. This is the book's eleventh year and we are hugely grateful to Ian and Queen Anne Press for publishing the charity sector's only hardback yearbook. Last year, the Trustees of Wooden Spoon, by way of thanks, voted unanimously to bestow Life Membership on Ian – needless to say he could not attend as he was fundraising for Spoon elsewhere. He may not consider himself a charmer but to us he is the best 'Artful Dodger' around!

ARE PROUD TO SUPPORT
WOODEN SPOON RUGBY WORLD '07

COMMENT & FEATURES

Male Imperando Summum Imperium Amittitur

by PAUL STEPHENS

'Robinson then accepted the job with the 2005 British & Irish Lions in New Zealand alongside Woodward. He should have gone with the England party to the Churchill Cup in Canada.'

With three disastrous seasons of audacious mismanagement and misplaced ambition behind them, the England hierarchy might well wish that the coming World Cup did not appear in 2007, but a year later. Perhaps by then, they could get properly organised and find a side capable of retaining the trophy they won so majestically in Australia in the autumn of 2003. If only it was a question of who deserves to gain a place in the party. If only.

Last season was not one which will linger long in the memory, but it has been a period when those with the shortest memories had the longest say in the possible return of Sir Clive Woodward to oversee the RFU's playing affairs from top to bottom. We all waited for the cream to be licked off this juicy trifle, but the whole business was tainted by myopia, for fear of alarming the many who are opposed implacably to such a disquieting action.

LEFT England coach Andy Robinson looks cheerful enough in Sydney in the summer. Will he still be smiling after England's performances in the 2007 World Cup?

FACING PAGE Sir Clive Woodward appears to be hallucinating at a league match between Southampton and Burnley in December 2005. Were he to be recalled as manager of the England rugby team, there could be plenty of supporters who will need to be forgiven for adopting a similar facial expression.

Andy Robinson did himself no favours with an alarming lack of judgment and the wildest decision-making. If that was not the case there would be no need for the Woodward call. Heaven help us if it happens, though the RFU's apparent faith in Robinson is neither bewildering nor does it offer contentment to those who follow England with unengaged confidence. For the time being – at least until the final of the next World Cup in France next autumn – Robinson's tenure remains unsound, if unchallenged.

But first let us look at the patchwork of errors made by Robinson since he initiated the riddle of mistakes. Retaining the coaching team chosen by Woodward, Robinson wanted to replace Joe Lydon. No chance. Jonny Wilkinson's injuries prevented him from accepting the captaincy. The Newcastle outside half missed most of last season, but is expected to return this term.

There was the decline of Jason Robinson, who chose to retire from international rugby at the end of the 2005 season. Billy Whizz was missed sorely. In November 2004, Henry Paul was taken off after 25 minutes in the match against Australia, when England were down 7-0. Paul soon vanished. Mathew Tait, picked at centre in place of Paul, was dumped by Gavin Henson in the opening match of the Six Nations Championship against Wales. Andy Robinson dropped Tait, and it took some time for the Newcastle back to recover. Robinson then accepted the job with the 2005 British & Irish Lions in New Zealand alongside Woodward. He should have gone with the England party to the Churchill Cup in Canada. His decision to accept his old boss's invitation cost him the chance to recover from a poor introductory Six Nations campaign. Greater familiarity with the lesser-known members of his squad might have brought substantial benefits for Andy Robinson.

Not content with these self-inflicted transgressions, Robinson was then summoned to suffer further misdemeanours; a project for which he could not have complained had he been overlooked. He reacted slowly to England's lack of attacking virtuosity by retaining Mike Tindall and Jamie Noon

we touch down all over the USA

▶▶ FLIGHTS FROM LONDON, MANCHESTER AND EDINBURGH

△Delta SKYTEAM

delta.com/uk

in the midfield, so denying more imaginative partners for Charlie Hodgson. Robinson then allowed Lawrence Dallaglio back into the squad, though not as captain. But the decision to allow him to replace Martin Corry at Murrayfield was absurd, while Matt Dawson's recall for Harry Ellis, and their constant replacement for one another, bordered on the insane given Dawson's imminent retirement from the game.

Was Robinson unlucky? I think not. All coaches have their black moments, and Robinson had plenty of those. In ordinary circumstances, Andy Robinson would have received the RFU's grateful thanks and been given plenty of freedom to undertake the gardening. It is as well to compare Robinson's first months with Woodward's calamitous start, when three Grand Slams were attended to shoddily, not to mention the World Cup quarter-final in Paris, when England were buried alive by South Africa.

But there is no time for a replacement to be chosen for Robinson. He needs help and sound advice. The new coaching team of Brian Ashton, Mike Ford and John Wells are a smart bunch. Far too smart for Woodward. Nick Mallett and Warren Gatland have already said no, while Springbok coach Jake White, inspired by the dwindling lack of enthusiasm for the England task and the refusal

of his home union to extend a contract until 2009, has recently added his name to the list. It might be an inspired choice, but would it not be better if the RFU considered John Prescott for the job?

Really, if there is no one suitable for the post, then nobody should be appointed. The RFU will save themselves plenty of money. Woodward is altogether too improvident. He spent a small fortune when last with England, and the British & Irish Lions tour to New Zealand was financially wasteful under Woodward's direction, as well as being a complete disaster from the playing point of view. Robinson and his cohorts ought to be allowed to get on with things in their own way. Should they get anywhere near the final of the World Cup in Paris next year, they would be forgiven for wallowing in self-congratulation.

RIGHT England debutant Mathew Tait is dumped unceremoniously by Gavin Henson at Cardiff in February 2005. Having decided that Tait was good enough to be picked for the Six Nations, Robinson promptly dropped the young centre after just one match. What a way to inspire confidence!

Firstly though, Robinson needs to take a close look at his selection policy. For this Ashton must be consulted. When Robinson chose Iain Balshaw for the two Tests in Australia, he probably telephoned Phil Davies, the former Leeds director of rugby, and asked him how Balshaw was playing. Balshaw having started only seven matches last season, Davies will, quite probably, have given him a glowing report. No good for England and not very useful for the player. Robinson should spend more time watching players. He visited games in the north of England on desolately few occasions last season.

Ashton, meanwhile, is much better versed and infinitely more complimentary about the youngsters who are ready to step up to international level. 'We have bags of young players who can make it,' Ashton told me before Bath's game at Northampton. 'Sure, they need experience, but every club has a few talented newcomers, and quite why we feel that the best way is to persevere with the old guard is beyond me.

'Charlie Hodgson has quickly proved himself to be a competent performer. Why can't Olly Morgan, Anthony Allen, James Bailey, Mark Foster, or Ryan Lamb of Gloucester be brought into the picture? There are some terrific forwards about. James Buckland and Michael Holford at Leicester for instance, where Tom Varndell has made such a good impression. Isn't Mathew Tait now the real thing?'

Ashton has since left Bath to join Robinson at Twickenham, but he needs to get his ideas across as forcefully and as soon as possible. The time has been reached where it has become impossible to include those not highly skilled or at the wrong end of their careers. Simon Shaw, Lawrence Dallaglio, Andy Goode, Ben Cohen, Mike Catt, Tom Voyce, Steve Thompson, Mike Tindall, Perry Freshwater and Martin Corry have all played their part with England, but now is the time for their departure.

For the second Test in Australia, Robinson made seven changes; one positional. Out went Olly Barkley, Louis Deacon and Alex Brown, flanker Magnus Lund, hooker Lea Mears and wing Voyce. Tait came in to play on the wing in a comprehensive unsettling exercise, which ended with England losing their fifth game in a row; the worst sequence for 23 years. This vapid nonsense must not be allowed to happen again. With some good fortune – they have another 12 internationals before the World Cup – underpinned by the trusty application of Robinson, Mike Ford, John Wells and Ashton, nor will it.

This supposes that the Premiership clubs get behind England, without the frustration of endless arguments about the release of players for international matches and other issues. With several high-ranking coaches passing up the opportunity to take over as the England supremo, is it any wonder that some players take shelter in a declining ambition to play for England? The remedy for this lies with the RFU Management Board, though only if they remember the perceptive proclamation by Publius Syrus: *Male imperando summum imperium amittitur*. The greatest empire may be lost by bad government.

Daniel Carter
the Perfect 10?

by RAECHELLE EDWARDS

'Stephen Larkham, Carter's opposition for the title of best number 10 in world rugby, describes the Kiwi as "the class five-eighth running around at the moment".'

It was one of the most complete performances in international rugby in recent times. Daniel Carter's tally of 33 points for the All Blacks against the British and Irish Lions in Wellington, New Zealand, on 2 July 2005, including two tries (one an exciting solo effort with a kick and chase into the corner), was an individual single-match record for points against the Lions. He ran, passed, chipped, kicked, tackled, set up his team-mates, scored his own tries and directed the play. A superstar of the game was born.

This was a rite of passage for Daniel Carter, whose commanding display proved that one man's brilliance could decimate one of the toughest sides in world rugby. His total of 44 points in two Tests leaves Carter just two points short of the most scored by any player in all Tests against the Lions (46 by Allan Hewson in four Tests in 1983).

His performance in the second Test of the series epitomised the New Zealand mindset of attacking rugby. His slick ball distribution kept the Lions constantly on the back foot. He was just

LEFT Daniel Carter in action against the Wallabies in August 2005. 'You are one pass away from the ball and it's also a leadership role where you can call the moves and that is something I enjoy.'

FACING PAGE Carter celebrates his second try of the second Test against the 2005 Lions at the Westpac Stadium, Wellington.

23, playing his twentieth Test, but only his sixth in the number 10 jersey. He gave everything a go, and it worked.

'Obviously it's the most unbelievable game I've had in the Black jersey,' Carter said. 'Everything seemed to flow. When you're scoring tries and throwing the ball around like that it's special. And when you're doing it with your mates, it's just great to play such good footie.

'I was very pleased with the way that game went.'

After the game All Black legend Grant Fox wrote: 'We have been blessed with some splendid [fly halves] over the years and I respect the likes of Andrew Mehrtens, Carlos Spencer and all those who came before. But I have no doubt Carter is going to be the greatest we've had.'

Carter brushes aside the compliments. 'I don't read too much into it, I play the game I love and do the best I can. People have their opinions.'

All Black coach Graham Henry summed up that match against the Lions when he said, 'Daniel Carter had an outstanding game. Goodness me.'

'The expectation is there but I don't make it a burden,' Carter said. 'I go out to play my game and read what happens in front of me. Obviously opportunities arise at times and it's a matter of making the most of them.'

It was fitting that Carter was named 2005 IRB Player of the Year. Now 24 years of age, his accolades also include being named New Zealand's Player of the Year in 2004 and 2005 and Super 12 Player of the Year in 2004. 'One of my dreams was to play for the All Blacks but it all happened

pretty quickly ... I still find it pretty hard to believe what I have achieved over the last couple of years.'

Along with the second Test against the Lions in 2005 Carter also rates his debut against Wales in 2003 as one of his most memorable games. 'It's a moment I will treasure for the rest of my life; it was such a special moment. A lot of hard work had gone into getting to that position, to finally pull on an All Black jersey. I will remember that day forever.' He scored 20 points in that game.

Carter has natural speed and athleticism. He is a good ball distributor, a reliable kicker, both in positional play and for goal, and has deceptive strength. He started his All Black career at inside centre and quickly moved to five-eighth (fly half), where he was instantly comfortable as the calm back-line general.

'Over the last year or two I have tried to cement my position in the number 10 jersey and I am enjoying that role. You are always in, or close to the action,' he said. 'You are one pass away from the ball and it's also a leadership role where you can call the moves and that is something I enjoy.

'It's been a big stepping stone for me to direct the play. Playing in a number 10 All Black jersey, that's your role. If you don't have that sort of capability things aren't going to function.'

As a runner, he is as good as Andrew Mehrtens or Carlos Spencer and is set to outshine both in terms of numbers of Test tries scored. But he is not a selfish player. 'It's just a matter of getting in those [try-scoring] situations and it helps that the team is playing some open rugby.

'We're throwing the ball around so there are opportunities to score tries. It's a bit of a bonus for me if I do reach a certain milestone but I'm just concentrating on each game individually and doing what I have to for the team.'

He is also on track to be as good a goal-kicker as Mehrtens or Grant Fox. He has already surpassed Crusaders predecessor Mehrtens's single-season record for the franchise of 206 points. Carter is cool under pressure. 'Goal-kicking is something I have always done and I love doing … you go through your usual routine.' Carter's father, whom he acknowledges as his greatest supporter, once gave him a set of goalposts for his birthday.

A born-and-bred Christchurch boy, Carter has developed through the ranks of the highly successful Canterbury Crusaders franchise where he had mentors of the calibre of Mehrtens, Justin Marshall and Aaron Mauger. 'We have had some pretty good success and I have been lucky enough to play with some quality players that I have learnt a lot from.'

Carter's ambition is achieving longevity at the top level. 'As a youngster you really want to play for the All Blacks and the challenge now is to become an All Black great. You can't just achieve that playing for a couple of seasons in the Black jersey, you have to be there playing for ten years.

'That's my ambition and it's tough with the young guys coming through, you always have to improve your skill base to keep your spot in the side.'

Stephen Larkham, Carter's opposition for the title of best number 10 in world rugby, describes the Kiwi as 'the class five-eighth running around at the moment'. Larkham, who has managed to achieve the longevity Carter is striving for, having played for the Australian side for ten years, has respect for Carter, who is eight years his junior. 'Dan Carter has been playing very well and he still has a bit of potential left in him. I think he'll be one of the key players in the World Cup in 2007,' Larkham said. 'He is a very naturally gifted player. He has a very good passing game. He has a very good kicking game and a very good running game,' he continued. 'He is very dangerous when he wants to run the ball and I think a lot of guys have fallen off tackles that they thought would be easier to make on him. He is very dangerous in attack.' But Larkham adds, 'Defensively he has a few weaknesses. In terms of missing tackles he is one of the highest in the New Zealand side so that's probably one area he's probably going to try to improve on before the World Cup.'

Carter also feels there is room for improvement in his game. 'With the All Blacks we all work on improving our strength … it's mainly the little things. In my position having vision and seeing space are pretty vital and I am always working on accurate passing.'

Carter says he learnt a lot as a 21-year-old when he played in his first World Cup in Australia. 'I got a taste for it in 2003 which makes me even more keen for this one … I learnt that in these tournaments you can go in with great form but on the day teams can pick themselves up.

'You need to concentrate on one match at a time and not look ahead to the final … it's hard to do that but you have to.

'We didn't do so well [in 2003] so I'll be doing everything I possibly can to be part of the All Black side to play in France.'

New Zealand haven't won a World Cup since David Kirk's men were victorious in the inaugural competition in 1987. 'It will be 20 years since we've won the World Cup so it's well overdue … It's something I'm really looking forward to.

'The coaches are trying to develop a lot of young guys so they can call on them and not lose anything … they have been working pretty hard for the last couple of years to build a team that is capable of winning the World Cup.'

Carter sees Australia, South Africa, England and France as the nations that New Zealand will be competing against for the Webb Ellis Cup. His performance is critical to the All Blacks' chances. Like other key players in the southern hemisphere teams, Carter is sure to be rested during the 2007 Super 14 series. 'DC', as he is known to his team-mates, is relaxed, enjoys a joke and having a good time. He says the best thing about playing international rugby is the places you travel to and the friends you make around the world.

Carter was voted New Zealand's sexiest man in the Durex Global Sex Survey in both 2004 and 2005. He is very marketable. In 2004 he fronted a billboard campaign throughout New Zealand for underwear manufacturer Jockey.

BELOW Carter is deceptively strong, as France's Nicolas Brusque finds out during the RWC 2003 third/fourth play-off.

Despite all the attention, Carter remains unaffected and away from rugby he enjoys 'hanging out with my friends that are not rugby players that I went to school and grew up with … it's quite refreshing. I like just chilling with them.'

At the World Cup in France, Carter will still only be 25 years of age, and the hopes of a nation will be resting on his broad shoulders.

Sale's Man
Saint-Andre Feeds the Sharks
by CHRIS HEWETT

"'Traditionalists don't like change, and the traditionalists at Sale had no faith in Philippe," he said, bluntly. "But I saw it as a no-brainer because I knew what he'd achieved…'"

O n the face of it, there is little onus on Philippe Saint-Andre to persuade anyone of anything, least of all his own merits as a rugby savant. As the scorer of the 'try from nowhere' against England on Grand Slam day in 1991 and the architect of the 'try from the end of the earth' against the All Blacks in Auckland three years later, he stands alongside Eric Bonneval, Patrice Lagisquet and Christophe Dominici as one of the finest French wings of the past 20 years. As the moderniser of Gloucester, the consolidator of Bourgoin and the strategist-in-chief of the new English champions, Sale, he cuts an entire Arctic Ocean's worth of ice as a coach, too.

And yet… When Brian Kennedy, the chairman and principal financier of Sale, framed his emotionally charged response to his club's victory over Leicester Tigers in the Guinness Premiership final in May, he made it abundantly clear that the decision to appoint Saint-Andre as director of rugby two-thirds of the way through the 2003-04 campaign was less than universally popular.

'Traditionalists don't like change, and the traditionalists at Sale had no faith in Philippe,' he said, bluntly. 'But I saw it as a no-brainer because I knew what he'd achieved during his time at Gloucester, and then back in France with Bourgoin. External circumstances had prevented him completing those jobs, but it was clear to me that here was a man who understood how to build winning teams. He surrounds himself with the right

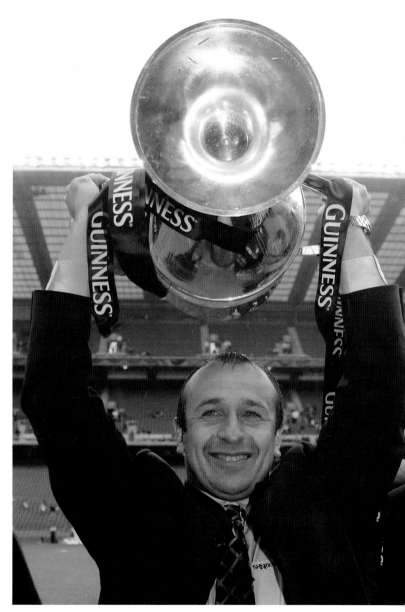

Tom Walkinshaw
Chairman
GRFC

Henry Paul

Philippe Saint-A...
Director of Ru...
GRFC

ABOVE Coach Saint-Andre, chairman Walkinshaw and captain Phil Vickery flank Henry Paul at the announcement of the latter's arrival at Gloucester from rugby league in 2001.

FACING PAGE Sale's piratical and influential back-rower Sebastien Chabal, brought to the club by Saint-Andre.

PREVIOUS PAGE Lifting the Guinness Premiership trophy as Sale's director of rugby in 2006.

coaching support, can articulate a clear plan of action, knows how to retain harmony in the group and does what he does with a rare passion. Above all, he hates losing.'

Kennedy is not particularly fond of losing either, and as a result it rarely happens. A sideways glance at his bank balance would surely confirm as much. He found himself in a tight corner over Saint-Andre, though. Jim Mallinder and Steve Diamond, two local products who had shared the England touring experience in Argentina in 1997, had proved mightily popular amongst the locals as they plotted and planned Sale's route into the elite echelon of the domestic game, and when the owner appointed the Frenchman to the rugby directorship, there were diehards on the terraces who took a very dim view of the decision. They wanted to know what the hell, and why. Why a change of coach in the first place? And if there had to be a change, for reasons they could not begin to fathom, why a foreign coach – especially one with an approach to the English language as interesting as Saint-Andre's?

Mallinder, a good-natured sort, played a straight bat and let the tough questions go past the outside edge and through to the 'keeper. Yes, he was sure he could work with Saint-Andre. No, he was not planning to jump ship. He was gone soon enough, however – a job with Brian Ashton's national academy was far too tempting to reject – so within a few weeks of taking charge, Saint-Andre was flying solo and dropping his little cluster bombs all over northwestern rugby by raiding the French market for top-quality forwards. Sebastien Bruno turned up, as did Sebastien Chabal. The locals remained suspicious. Yet these two would prove magnificent acquisitions, providing Sale with the backbone they required to win the European Challenge Cup in 2005. By then, Saint-Andre had convinced the vast majority of his sporting public that he was a force for good.

Thus encouraged, Saint-Andre went Tricolore-fishing a second time and came home with Daniel Larrechea, Valentin Courrent and Lionel Faure. Each and every one of them contributed, as Bruno and Chabal continued to do. Larrechea, recruited from Bayonne, was probably the pick of the Sale backs as they made their early-season statements last autumn; Courrent, signed from Brive, played important roles in both half-back positions, not least when Charlie Hodgson was away with England; Faure, brought over from Pau, was a tad too violent to begin with, but the prop more than paid his

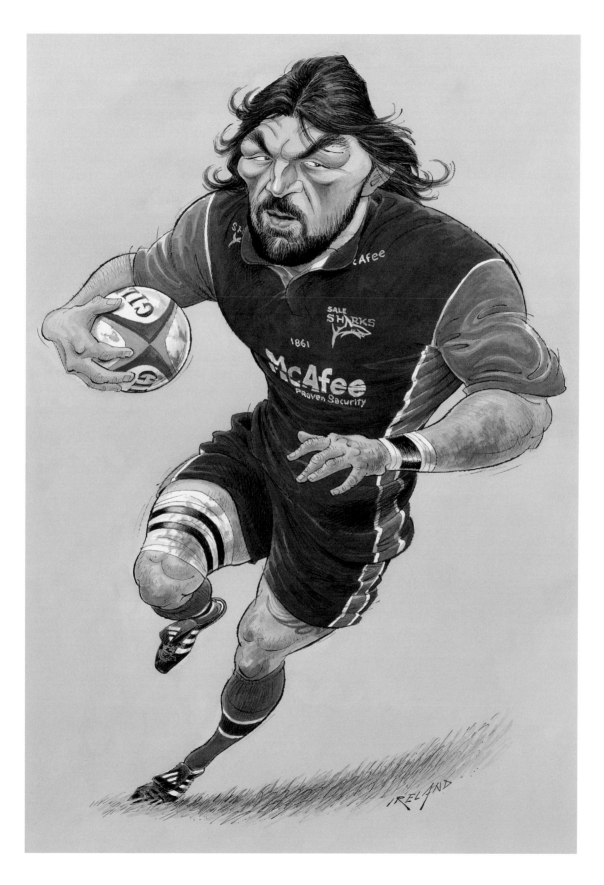

way when Saint-Andre lost the mammoth Andrew Sheridan to injury and needed someone mean to shore up the loose-head side of the scrum.

The surprising aspect of all this was that anyone should have been surprised, for Saint-Andre had taken Gloucester through the gears and up to speed in similar fashion during his stay at Kingsholm, which ended a couple of years before he surfaced at Sale. The Cherry and Whites did not land a championship under his stewardship, but they reached a Heineken Cup semi-final – no mean achievement for a side wholly unschooled in the complex art of top-class European competition. It was there that the Frenchman established his modus operandi, scouring his home country for the Olivier Azams and Patrice Collazos and Dimitri Yachvilis. Indeed, Yachvili may be the most prescient signing ever made by a Premiership coach. Saint-Andre spotted him as a nobody, playing minor-league rugby for the Paris University club. Now with Biarritz – and, of course, the French national team – he is among the finest players in the world, in any position.

Saint-Andre is living proof that the real tradition of French rugby is not the tradition the English imagine it to be. For him, the beast is more important than the beauty. 'I played my international rugby with Serge Blanco and Philippe Sella, with the Lafonds and Sadournys and Camberaberos,' he once said. 'These were great footballers. Yet we were happy to wait for an hour without doing anything, because we knew it was vital that the forwards did the bad things first.' The bad things. These Saint-Andre understands as well as any plug-ugly forward-turned-coach. So deep is his understanding, in fact, that he comes across as a frustrated prop who would rather have participated in the scrum from the end of the earth than created the try from it.

As Jason White, the Scotland blind-side flanker who played such an epic hand in helping Sale to their first league title, pointed

> **BELOW** More beast than beauty? Saint-Andre puts in a big tackle for France v Wales in 1995.

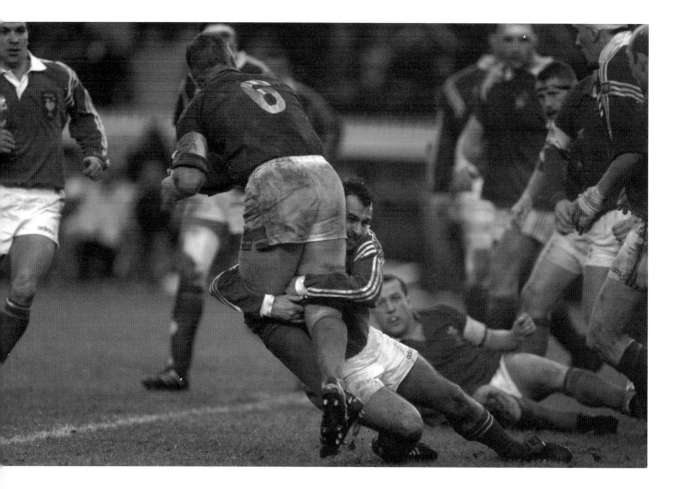

out just before the final with Leicester: 'I'm playing in a really strong, dominant pack for the first time in my career. Everyone who knows rugby understands that Scottish packs are invariably lighter than their opponents, and that consequently they play in a particular style, fighting for every scrap of possession that might be going and trying to make the most of whatever comes to hand. Sale are different. They had this reputation for playing free-flowing rugby through a great back

division, but Philippe saw that to be successful, we would have to beef ourselves up and mix it up front. We have achieved that this season. I'm playing on the front foot here, and it makes life easier.'

There is no resistance to Saint-Andre at Sale now. On his own admission, he found it difficult to communicate his ideas at Gloucester, partly because he did not work sufficiently hard at his English – he spent several years referring to the groundsman as 'man with beard', if Kingsholm legend is to be believed – and partly because he insisted on surrounding himself with French colleagues, most notably Laurent Seigne, a fearsome denizen of the Tricolore front row of yore. This does not excuse, or fully explain, Gloucester's treatment of him towards the end of his tenure – Tom Walkinshaw, the chairman, described him as 'the best coach this club has had by a country mile' and then refused to discuss a new contract – but the brief move back to France with Bourgoin probably gave him the time and space he needed to refine his ideas on Premiership rugby. When Sale came knocking, he knew precisely what needed to be done, and by whom. He still speaks in Franglais, but he makes himself understood.

It is perfectly possible that France will come knocking the minute Bernard Laporte steps down as national coach after the 2007 World Cup. Saint-Andre believes there are more experienced, and better qualified, successors already working in Le Championnat, singling out both Lagisquet of Biarritz and Guy Noves of Toulouse. Even so, his name will be considered. Unlike his fellow Test wings, he knows what it is to embrace rugby in all its cosmopolitanism and make full sense of a foreign culture, and if he is more than capable of Noves-style spontaneous combustion when things go wrong on the field, he is sufficiently urbane and charming away from the weekend hothouse to negotiate a course through the politics of the game in his homeland.

'Yes, the French probably will come after him,' sighed Kennedy at Twickenham back in May. 'If they do, I'll do everything in my power to keep him here.' Having backed a winner against the odds, he is not of a mind to open the stable door.

200 Years On
the Webb Ellis Saga

by CHRIS THAU

'The claim that Webb Ellis started the distinctive running feature of the game was made in 1876, some four years after his death, in the Rugby School magazine *The Meteor*.'

The 200th anniversary of William Webb Ellis' birthday on 24 November 2006, as well as the recent publicity surrounding the town of Menton, his final resting place on the French Riviera, has reignited the debate over the former Rugby School pupil, who reportedly 'with a fine disregard for the rules of football as played in his time, first took the ball in his arms and ran with it ...'

The claim that Webb Ellis started the distinctive running feature of the game was made in 1876, some four years after his death, in the Rugby School magazine *The Meteor*. The originator of the story was a local antiquarian, author and school benefactor, Matthew Bloxam, himself a former Rugby School pupil. In October 1876 Bloxam wrote to *The Meteor* that he had learnt from an unnamed source that the change from a kicking game to a handling game had '... originated with a town boy or foundationer of the name of Ellis, William Webb Ellis'.

LEFT The statue at Rugby School that commemorates the origins of the game of rugby. It was unveiled in 1997 by Jeremy Guscott.

FACING PAGE One of a set of drawings from 1845 by Rugby pupil Charles Harcourt Chambers to illustrate the rules, set down for the first time that year.

PAGE 34 A watercolour of a football match in progress on the Close, Rugby School, in the 1850s.

worked out of a "scrummage" – "dropping the island goal"

In December 1880, in a subsequent letter to *The Meteor*, Bloxam elaborated on the original story as follows: 'A boy of the name Ellis – William Webb Ellis – a town boy and a foundationer, … whilst playing Bigside at football in that half-year, caught the ball in his arms. This being so, according to the then rules, he ought to have retired back as far as he pleased, without parting with the ball, for the combatants on the opposite side could only advance to the spot where he had caught the ball, and were unable to rush forward till he had either punted it or had placed it for some one else to kick, for it was by means of these placed kicks that most of the goals were in those days kicked, but the moment the ball touched the ground the opposite side might rush on. Ellis, for the first time, disregarded this rule, and on catching the ball, instead of retiring backwards, rushed forwards with the ball in his hands towards the opposite goal, with what result as to the game I know not, neither do I know how this infringement of a well-known rule was followed up, or when it became, as it is now, a standing rule.'

These are the only accounts mentioning William Webb Ellis as the originator of the running game, and over the years Bloxam's version of the events was challenged and his credibility questioned, as the identity of the source of his story remained a closely guarded secret. Some historians went even further and dismissed his account as a myth or pure fiction. Additionally, the fact that the running game did not become a feature of Rugby School football until the late 1830s has been used as evidence that the actual event was apocryphal. In order to shed further light on the Webb Ellis mystery, it is worthwhile to examine both the possible source of Bloxam's account as well as the way the rules of football evolved at the school.

Matthew Bloxam, the author of the letter to *The Meteor*, was the second youngest of the six Bloxam brothers, sons of the Reverend Richard Rouse Bloxam, an assistant master at Rugby between 1790 and 1828. All six Bloxams attended the school and two of them – the youngest, John Rouse, and the second youngest, Matthew Holbeche – were contemporaries of Webb Ellis, though both were older than him, by one year and two years respectively.

Matthew's reluctance to disclose the origin of the information about Webb Ellis may well have to do with the source itself. This could have been either one of his brothers or possibly his own father, who was one of Ellis' masters, since the brothers also seem to have been privy to some rumour and conjecture about Ellis' school work. A letter written in April 1822 by Thomas Lawrence Bloxam to his younger brother Andrew is quite significant in this respect. In it Thomas wrote to Andrew about the annual race at school, describing Ellis' failure to win and, significantly, an alleged malpractice at Latin. While it is clear that Thomas watched the race as an eyewitness, his comments about Ellis' Latin work must have come from another source. Here is an extract from the letter: 'Ellis got the

Wooden Spoon, in plain terms was the last Horse that was placed. He had taken for his Latin Motto for the Latin Prize "Dux Femina facti", which the Masters thought was a broad hint that his mother had been helping him in the composition.'

It is quite unlikely that in such tightly knit society any unusual event would have passed unnoticed ('There is no Rugby News afloat, nor have there been any Rows this half year ...', wrote Thomas). For this reason William Webb Ellis' 'fine disregard for the rules of football' displayed in a Bigside match, arguably one of the most significant sporting and social events in the school, would almost certainly have been noted and debated at the Bigside Levee (meeting of senior boys to discuss football) as well as in the Bloxam family. Matthew Bloxam, who was 18 at the time of Ellis' alleged exploit and lived in Rugby with his family, must have heard about it from a number of sources, one of which could have been his father, which may explain his reluctance to disclose.

Another aspect that requires scrutiny is the way the rules of football at Rugby School evolved over centuries, from the rough and tumble of village football as played in the early days to the increasingly 'scientific' game of the late 19th century. The rules of football at Rugby School were written down for the first time in 1845 at the initiative of the then head boy, Isaac Gregory Smith, and running with the ball was one of them. Yet it is known that running with the ball had become common practice at Bigside matches before that – about 10 to 15 years after 1823 – though there is no explanation of how this happened nor any historical evidence. Seemingly every football rule changed slowly through the endeavour of generation after generation of Rugby School pupils. This is why the reported 'run' of William Webb Ellis is unlikely to have had an immediate impact on the game. Perhaps running with the ball was tried time and again and its merits and demerits debated, though never recorded, at the Bigside Levee.

In order to investigate the circumstances of the William Webb Ellis exploit a committee of Old Rugbeians, H.F. Wilson, H.H. Child, A.G. Guillemard and H.L. Stephen, was appointed in 1895. The committee arrived at the following conclusions, containing (below in italics) some of the comments made by Bloxam in 1876:

• In 1820 the game played at Rugby School had more features resembling soccer than rugby.

• The innovation of running with the ball was introduced sometime between 1820 and 1830.

• The author of the 'innovation' was probably Mr W. Webb Ellis – whose *unfair practices* were the *subject of general remark*.

Building for the Big One
Wales and RWC 2007

by STEPHEN JONES

'Jenkins realises full well that the heartbeat of Welsh rugby does not lie in an office in Cardiff but in the fields and highways and byways out in the country.'

There is a view that the glorious Welsh Grand Slam triumph in 2005 may turn out to be a one-off, almost a cruel hoax. The dip in performance in the 2006 RBS Six Nations Championship and the heavy defeat of Wales by Argentina in the summer of 2006 completed what amounted to a staggering decline in results.

Indeed, there can be no real sense of optimism on the surface as yet. England are also struggling, and since they have Samoa in their pool in the World Cup while Wales have to take on Fiji, it is by no means out of the question that a South Seas upset of gigantic proportions could even be looming.

But unless something really catastrophic befalls England and Wales, then the two old rivals will meet in the quarter-finals of RWC 2007, and frankly the attention of everyone in Welsh rugby in any professional capacity must now be focused on producing a fit, revived and outstanding team to win that quarter-final. An appearance by Wales in the semi-finals would represent a triumph, would rock English rugby to its foundations – and anything after that would be a bonus for Wales.

Where to start? It still seems unbelievable that Wales could find the first coach for nearly 30 years with the ability to guide them to a Grand Slam, only to jettison him months afterwards. But the best news is that Wales have resisted the temptation to install a foreign lame duck, who would have carried on a rather sad line. They have done the right thing in appointing Gareth Jenkins, and it will be fascinating to see if, as expected, Jenkins can revive the team with new passion, new direction, new organisation and new attacking ideas. These are areas in which he has been successful, albeit with a limited budget, for some time.

Better still, Jenkins realises full well that the heartbeat of Welsh rugby does not lie in an office in Cardiff but in the fields and highways and byways out in the country. He will surely arrest the decline of top domestic rugby in the country, and even though he is now national coach he will surely be keen to set professional rugby free, rather than to subjugate it to the Welsh Rugby Union – who have made such an horrendous hash of it.

You slightly fear for Jenkins in the build-up period at his disposal. He faces Australia, the Pacific Islands and New Zealand in a difficult autumn series. However, the rampaging shortcomings of the Celtic League as a competition, the fact that so many competing teams are so half-hearted about it, robs Jenkins of a sustained series of red-hot matches, vital to knock his men into shape and to achieve match fitness for a host of injured stars.

However, it is easy to become too depressed and it is easy to forget that one of the overwhelming factors in the decline of Wales last season was a dreadful series of serious injuries. It is important to remember that the Welsh team which took part in the 2006 Six Nations was actually a second team and that the brave young men who wore the red jersey in Argentina were a third team. Good luck to them, but it really is no surprise that they were not up to it.

There is no guarantee that all the injured legions will be fit to resume and will be restored to their best form. Nor is there any guarantee, obviously, that the horrible injury jinx will not strike again. But let us assume that most of the injured men do return. If you add to the Welsh pack players such as Chris Horsman, Brent Cockbain, Ryan Jones, Luke Charteris and Gethin Jenkins, then you are improving the situation clean out of sight. All of these potential world-class forwards either suffered injury last season or simply lost conditioning.

In particular, the effervescent Jones will be desperate to re-emphasise the magnificent form he showed against all the odds when playing for the Lions in New Zealand in 2005. Meanwhile,

Private Banking & Property Finance | Asset Management | Investment Banking | Treasury & Specialised Finance

Instinctive supporters

Investec is proud to support the Wooden Spoon. We are a specialist banking group offering private banking & property finance, asset management, investment banking and treasury and specialised finance. For more information please call **020 7597 4000** or visit our website **www.investec.com**

Out of the Ordinary

⊕ Investec

Horsman will also be anxious to show his true self. He certainly has the potential to become one of the world's most formidable props.

In the back division, players such Dwayne Peel, Gareth Thomas, Mark Jones and Kevin Morgan are expected to be fit in good time for the autumn matches, and here again it is possible that the team could be galvanised out of sight if they all find their true form.

Perhaps the two most anxiously awaited revivals, however, are those of Gavin Henson and Tom Shanklin in the centre. That pair were the key to the Wales Grand Slam. Shanklin, still struggling with a knee injury which could yet mark the end of his career, was positively dazzling in the Slam, and supporters of both Cardiff and Wales will be praying for a recovery every bit as fervently as England cricket followers are praying for the knee of Michael Vaughan.

Henson's ascent to true world class depends not only on his own dedication and his own ability to distinguish show business from professional sport. A lot also depends on the ability of Jenkins, and the Welsh players and supporters, to nurture, and have sympathy for, an absolutely magnificent all-round talent. Sir Clive Woodward on the Lions tour was by no means the first coach to misunderstand and to misuse Henson. Let us hope that Henson will prove ripplingly fit for the new international campaign, to give European rugby a polished gem.

Overall, I just have the suspicion that Wales are indeed on the way up. It is true that the team's medical and remedial staff will be as important as the players in the near future. But there is a richness and all-round talent about the potential Welsh squad which, all other things being equal, could see them develop into a very fine team.

Certainly, time is short. Jenkins, if he has any aspirations to a semi-final in France next year, will be looking for victory over Australia and the Pacific Islands, and will be looking to be at least ferociously competitive against New Zealand. He will want Wales to be playing so well before the New Zealand clash in the autumn that the All Blacks do not dare to leave out any key players, something they have tended to do of late when facing matches in which they are all but assured of victory.

The squad has a decent balance of power and invention. Jenkins must not fall into the same trap as England, who appear to have sacrificed power and weight up front and throughout the team to chase some misguided notion of attacking rugby. Wales, perhaps anchored by the likes of Horsman, can certainly field a pack outstanding in the primary phases. And with the cutting edges of Peel, Thomas and Henson behind the scrum, then there is a happy prospect of successful attacking rugby, rather than the mere promise of it.

Who knows, Wales may yet find ways to scupper their own progress. Their domestic rugby, even though augmented by exciting overseas signings, is still flabby and unfocused. But they have a pool of players to usher in better days, and even to make themselves a decent long shot for the Big One in France next year.

RIGHT It is expected that Dwayne Peel will be fit once again by the autumn to provide a cutting edge behind the Wales scrum.

Jason White
High-Impact Player

by JILL DOUGLAS

'Scotland's commitment was typified by their captain's devastating tackle on Joe Worsley as England's final attack was thwarted.'

Jason White learned of the impact he could make on the rugby field at an early age. While playing for Aberdeen Wanderers at Under 14 level, he tackled the biggest, toughest boy in the opposing team, who promptly left the pitch in tears. These days the Scotland captain has a fearsome reputation as one of the most physical and unforgiving tacklers in the game; he has nurtured and developed his talent for reducing grown men to tears.

'It's something that comes naturally,' says White. 'I realised in my very first match that I had a knack for it, it's something I can bring to a game and now I work hard on my strength because I know of the impact it can have.'

That impact was demonstrated in style during the Six Nations when White led Scotland to a top-three finish, their best performance since the championship grew from five participants to six and exceeding all expectations. The hard, physical nature of Scotland's game proved vital in their memorable wins over France and England at Murrayfield. Add to that a Guinness Championship win with his English club side Sale Sharks and a hatful of prestigious awards and it amounts to a remarkable season for the gritty loose forward who played almost 40 games over the course of the year.

'It really started at the tail end of the previous season when I was a late call-up for the Lions to New Zealand.

'It had been a goal to make the tour and I was disappointed when I missed out, so to join the team and play in the last midweek game in Auckland was brilliant.

'It was a really positive experience and the season just went on from there.'

Pre-season training in France with his Sale team-mates led to a session of goal-setting. 'We wanted to qualify out of our group in the Heineken Cup and make it into the top two in the Guinness Premiership and make the end-of-season semi-finals. We got to the top in the first few weeks of the season and stayed there.

'As far as Scotland was concerned, well J.P. [Jon Petrie] had been captain the previous season but was out with a dislocated shoulder so I knew there was an outside chance I might get the chance. I'd played under Frank Hadden at Under 16 level and with Caley [Caledonian] Reds so he knew me reasonably well.'

ABOVE Robert Sidoli of Wales gets first-hand experience of a Jason White special during the 2006 Six Nations match at the Millennium Stadium.

FACING PAGE Jason White, Scotland captain, raises high the Calcutta Cup after his side's 18-12 win over England.

White led his country for the first time against Argentina at Murrayfield in November in a game they ultimately lost, though one in which they did enough to prove to the Scottish public that this was a group of players who had turned a corner. They went on to beat Samoa and battled hard against a New Zealand team who were gunning for a tour Grand Slam.

Meanwhile, the domestic season rolled on, with Sale enjoying continued success in what is recognised as one of the toughest leagues in the professional game.

'If you are not playing at 100 per cent in a game then any team at the bottom can beat any team at the top on any given weekend. I think that's the hardest element of the Premiership, there just aren't any easy games.

'Winning the Premiership was such a highlight. It was brilliant to see Manchester come out on top of all the established clubs in England. There's a great combination of home-grown players here and Philip Saint-Andre has brought in top-quality players from France and elsewhere to get the right balance.'

Of course there was the small matter of the RBS Six Nations to contest before White and his Sale team-mates could make it to Twickenham for their championship final. Scotland were close favourites for the Wooden Spoon prior to the opening weekend of matches, but the odds were changed dramatically after their thrilling win over France at Murrayfield.

'We're always comfortable to go in as underdogs and I think we played the French at the best time. They'd only had a couple of days to train together because of the nature of their busy league schedule. This was my fiftieth cap, a huge day for me and the first time I'd captained Scotland in the Six Nations.

'As the clock ticked down we just had to keep going, the crowd were just brilliant, we scored a couple of good tries with Sean Lamont going over after a big forward effort. It was the best possible start to the campaign.'

An outnumbered Scotland then lost to Wales in Cardiff before preparing to take on England in their only other home game of the Six Nations. 'We really felt we had a chance to do something special. We knew they liked to keep hold of the ball and grind out the win so we talked about smashing them in the tackle.'

LEFT Sale forwards Jason White (left), Ignacio Fernandez Lobbe and Chris Jones go walkabout after the Sharks' victory over Leicester Tigers in the 2006 Guinness Championship final at Twickenham.

FACING PAGE White on the rampage. The Sale flanker takes on Biarritz's Petru Balan and Jerome Thion during the 2005-06 Heineken Cup clash in San Sebastian.

White earned his first cap for Scotland in their shock win over England in 2000, but this was a sweeter victory for the Aberdonian. 'In 2000 it was our last game of the tournament after a run of defeats. The weather was atrocious which played a part and it was to simply salvage something from the season.

'In this year's win the weather wasn't a factor and it wasn't a one-off victory, it came off the back of another good performance. We backed it up after beating another of the top teams.'

Scotland's commitment was typified by their captain's devastating tackle on Joe Worsley as England's final attack was thwarted. The two home wins and a victory in Italy finally gave Scottish fans something to cheer about, the first few positive steps for Scottish rugby in some considerable time. 'The players are working really hard to play for each other and instil confidence. We've shown there are great players in Scotland, but for us to have success, we need to have all of our best 15 players on the pitch and perform as best as we possibly can. It needs to be full on, we need to give it everything just to compete with the other sides.

'We didn't do that in the first tour match in South Africa, it wasn't good enough. But the tour was great for the younger guys and a real learning curve.'

White toured as the newly named Scottish PRA (Professional Rugby Association) Player of the Year, and was also the first Scot to receive the prestigious Player of the Year award from the corresponding body in England. 'It was voted for by my peers so that made it all the more special. One or two of the English guys must have voted for me so to earn their respect means a lot. It has been a special year.'

So what does 2006-07 hold for the 28-year-old? 'Personally I have to look at the season that's gone as a base level and build on that. I am motivated to perform as well as I can for Sale and Scotland and of course with the World Cup to come, it's a big year.'

No one will dispute that Scotland have some hard months ahead, but with White at the helm, leading by example, they might just prove to be a surprise hit.

BEHIND SCOTTISH RUGBY.

INTERNATIONAL SCENE

A Magnificent Celebration
the Hong Kong Sevens

by IAN ROBERTSON

'The most significant aspect of the Hong Kong tradition is the fact that the "haves" and "have nots" of world rugby eat at the same table for one glorious weekend every year.'

This was, as always, a magnificent celebration of all that is best in sevens rugby. But in 2006 it was a very special celebration – the 30th birthday of this wonderful extravaganza. Cathay Pacific have proudly sponsored from way back, right through to the new IRB version of this great tournament.

The most significant aspect of the Hong Kong tradition is the fact that the 'haves' and 'have nots' of world rugby eat at the same table for one glorious weekend every year. Since 1976 it has always been thus, and hopefully it always will be.

In the initial pool stages, the minnows of the global game swim in the same tank as the sharks. So China found themselves facing South Africa and Wales in Pool C and inevitably they capitulated. But they regrouped and went on to win the final of the Bowl, beating Taiwan.

Little Sri Lanka were overwhelmed by both France and Australia in Pool E, but they had, as Andy Warhol would have said, their 15 minutes of fame when they beat the USA in the quarter-finals of the Bowl.

Wales, the Grand Slam Six Nations champions of 2005, slumped horribly in 2006 but after losing to South Africa in Pool C, they recovered to beat Portugal in the quarter-finals of the Plate competition, Canada in the semi-finals and then Kenya in the final.

Scotland had their best tournament for many years, rattling up 82 points against Singapore and 52 points against Japan to reach the quarter-finals of the main Cup competition. They lost to Fiji there, but acquitted themselves really well.

The pursuit of the Cup evolved into exactly the fierce competition which everyone anticipated. Three teams stood out – Fiji, the leaders of the IRB World Sevens rankings; New Zealand, the winners of the 2006 Commonwealth Games gold medal in Melbourne just two weeks previously; and England, the silver medal runners-up in Melbourne. These three teams were determined to battle it out for the Cup, although it has to be said that England very nearly came a cropper in a thrilling quarter-final tie against Samoa.

The tie began disastrously for England, with both Keneti Tofilau and Uale Mai scoring tries in the opening two minutes. Both conversions were missed, but a deficit of 10-0 was not the start England had wanted. England managed one converted try to trail 10-7 at half-time, and another converted try at the start of the second half gave England a lead of 14-10 and the initiative.

ABOVE England's Mathew Tait lays hold of Uale Mai of Samoa during the quarter-finals of the Cup competition. A ruling by a touch judge disallowed a last-ditch Samoa try and put England through to the semis.

FACING PAGE England celebrate with the trophy after beating Fiji 26-24 in the final.

However, the real drama was to unfold the moment the full-time hooter went to end the match with the ball in play near the touch line, just inside the England 22-metre line. Samoa recycled the ball and created an overlap 60 metres wide to score what seemed the winning try in the corner. At this moment the Fates came to England's rescue. Just as they thought they were out of the tournament, the touch judge on the side where the move started had his flag aloft. He decreed the Samoans had a toenail in touch at the very start of the final move and the referee had no option but to disallow the Samoan try. Such is the fine line between defeat and victory. England cruised past South Africa 24-0 in the semi-finals to reach the final.

The other semi-final between Fiji and New Zealand was equally one-sided. In a blistering first half the Fijians ran in four tries, which were all converted by the world's most famous sevens player, Waisale Serevi. Twenty-eight points to nil – end of contest. Fiji eased off in the second half to let New Zealand score two tries but then ran in a fifth score at the end to win 35-10. Exit the Commonwealth Games champions.

The final was sporting theatre at its very best. In the first half England led 12-7 with tries from Tom Varndell and Ben Gollings. England looked as if they had built up an unassailable lead when Mathew Tait, a player of tremendous potential, scored a third try to make it 19-7. But the Fijians

suddenly hit top form and ran in three tries in the space of four minutes to swoop into a 24-19 lead. With exactly one minute left, England conceded a penalty on the Fiji 22. Serevi kicked to touch, 40 seconds to go, and Fiji won the line out. That seemed to be it. Surely they could keep possession of the ball for 30 seconds and then kick it into touch. They drove into England to set up a ruck but lost the ball. The hooter went for full time with England in possession. England launched two attacks; Fiji defended. With the third piece of recycled possession, living on borrowed time, Ben Gollings created space to score the winning try. The capacity crowd of 40,000 had enjoyed another fantastic end to the Hong Kong Sevens – the best sevens tournament in the world year after year.

ABOVE China are jubilant after beating Taiwan 47-0 in the final of the Bowl.

FACING PAGE Alando Soakai looks determined as New Zealand take on Fiji in the Cup semis. Fiji triumphed nonetheless to face England in the final.

Of course, the Hong Kong Sevens is not only about rugby. It is a whole week of festivities, with the annual tens tournament kick-starting the action with two days of rugby at the Hong Kong football club. Teams fly in from all over the world and a big crowd watched two sides from New Zealand contest the final. March wasn't too bad a month for the All Blacks, whose 15-a-side team are Tri-Nations champions and red-hot favourites for the 2007 Rugby World Cup. They finished first and second in the Hong Kong Tens and they won the Commonwealth Games gold medal.

Finally, what makes the Cathay Pacific Sevens in Hong Kong so very special is the crowd. The fans dress up in all sorts of amazing kit and not only enter into the spirit of the weekend, they actually create that great atmosphere. Our pictorial tribute overleaf bears witness to that.

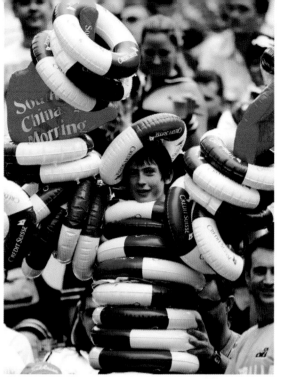

New experiences keep us young and maintain our sense of wonder. Only by travelling can we ex

live in. Move farther with Cathay Pacific to over 90 destinations worldwide. You never know v

call 020 8834 8888 or visit www.cathaypacific.co.uk

Move farther

many cultures and people that make up the world we
'll see until you're there. To fly Cathay Pacific,

A New Departure
Japan Change Direction

by CHRIS THAU

'The epitome of the "old Japan style" was the sensational demolition of the Junior All Blacks in 1968, with Yoshihiro "Demi" Sakata ... scoring four magnificent tries.'

The appointment of former La Rochelle and France scrum half Jean-Pierre Elissalde as coach of Japan is arguably one of the most surprising and perhaps significant coaching appointments of recent years. This is not only a new coaching job for the talented Frenchman, father to current French scrum half Jean-Baptiste Elissalde and son of the legendary La Rochelle coach Arnaud Elissalde, but also signals a major shift in Japanese rugby, both in terms of playing philosophy and practical approach. After many years of trying to emulate first the British, then the Antipodean coaching structures and philosophies, Japan have suddenly changed course and opted for French expertise. The appointment of Elissalde, who has yet to prove himself at top international level, must be seen within the wider context of a return to the roots of the Japanese rugby culture, the approach that brought Japan both success and recognition in the 1960s.

'I want Japan to play the kind of rugby they are capable of, not to imitate the physical European approach. Japan, while retaining all aspects related to the

LEFT Japan head coach and former France scrum half Jean-Pierre Elissalde watches his side defeat Korea 50-14 in an RWC 2007 Asian zone qualifier in Tokyo in April. Elissalde wants to see Japan play a style of rugby that suits their strengths of 'elusiveness and quick reaction'.

physicality of rugby, must play a game in which they use their elusiveness and quick reaction to good effect,' Elissalde said.

The epitome of the 'old Japan style' was the sensational demolition of the Junior All Blacks in 1968, with Yoshihiro 'Demi' Sakata, the electric winger, scoring four magnificent tries. Sakata, nowadays a professor at Osaka University, explains:

'In 1966, before the 1968 tour to New Zealand, Japan formed its first-ever national representative squad. We, and in fact Japanese rugby as a whole, were extremely fortunate to have the services of an excellent coach, Mr Ohnishi. He was constantly thinking about strategies and tactics that would make the most of Japanese rugby players' size, speed, techniques and unique qualities. He was constantly devising strategies to maximise the qualities of Japanese players against teams made up of larger, slower players.

'At the time of the 1968 match against the Junior All Blacks, the Japanese national team players' average height was 171.5cm, and average weight was 72.5kg. Against that, the Junior All Blacks averaged 181cm and 87kg respectively [an average of 10cm taller and 15kg heavier]. It was distinctive Japanese tactics that overcame this size and weight handicap. The players used techniques to overcome larger opponents, and I think that was a major factor that drove the improvement in Japanese rugby during that era. Using clever tactics, players put all of their skills to good use, sharpening their competitiveness.

'After that, what happened was a growing desire to increase the size of the players in Japanese teams. Tall and heavy players began to enter the national team in large numbers, which led to a loss of identity, a loss of our unique style and approach, which made the difference. The new, larger players were unable to carry out the distinctive, nimble moves of previous years. Thus, the team went on losing, and the solution seemed to bring even bigger players, which in turn led to an increased loss of agility and nimbleness. I honestly believe that the national team grew weaker as the tactics that suited the smaller Japanese players were no longer used.'

The new-look Japan were recently offered a chance to test the new approach in a high-quality playing environment, against the formidable Junior All Blacks and three South Pacific islands – Samoa, Fiji and Tonga – in the so-called Pacific 5 Nations tournament, sponsored by the International Rugby Board as part of its campaign to increase standards in the second-tier nations. Though they finished last, with four defeats out of four matches, Japan looked increasingly competent and confident, as the Elissalde medication started to have an effect on the overall playing style. One of the first to benefit from the new approach during the build-up to the Pacific 5 Nations was the new Sakata, Daisuke Ohata, the new holder of the world Test-try-scoring record.

A hat-trick of tries against Georgia in a warm-up Test at Hanazono Stadium in Ohata's birthplace of Osaka broke the record held by Australia's David Campese. The new mark of 65 tries in 55 matches bettered Campese's record of 64 in 101 Tests, still an Australian record.

'I am very happy to break the record and would like to thank my team-mates, my coaches and of course the great players before me that made this possible,' said Ohata at the end of a special ceremony at which he received a special award of 1 million yen from the Japan Rugby Football Union and a special gold-striped shirt to mark the occasion.

The 31-year-old Kobe Steel winger commenced his try-scoring rampage with a hat-trick of tries against Korea in 1996, though he had given warning of his awesome finishing power when he scored four tries in a non-cap international against Thailand at the 15th Asian Championship. He has scored a total of 21 tries in five non-cap matches, which would increase his world record tally to 86. Interviewed two weeks before his record-breaking day, Ohata had this to say:

'I have heard all about the wonderful players who have represented Japan in the past, I think that there is great merit in the legacy that they have left us. Similar to Sakata who scored four tries against the Junior All Blacks, and Yoshida who scored a try for the World XV so too I want to achieve results, and leave a legacy for players to come.

'With the type of play that I do, I do get a lot of pleasure from scoring tries. But rugby is a team game, a team with many players in it, and it is fun just to take part, to meet people, things like that.

'I started playing rugby because of my father. He played rugby at high school, and influenced me to take up the game. It was always a sport that was close to me, and I started playing in the third year of elementary school. From there, I wanted to play in a team that would reach the national High

School Tournament finals at Hanazono. But there are many strong teams in Osaka, so I joined a new school, choosing it so we could build up a team and aim for Hanazono our way. I played for three years at high school, and was lucky to be surrounded by wonderful coaches. And I was selected for the Japanese high school representative team. I wanted to carry on with rugby at a university in the Kansai, and put in four years of hard training at Kyoto Sangyo University. Then, when I was in the third year at university, I was lucky enough to be chosen for the full Japanese national team for the first time. This will now be my tenth year playing for the national team, and I believe that I now have the experience to adapt to the players around me without cramping my own style.

'For me, breaking the record is not the final goal in my career, if I can break the record soon, I want to take it as far as I can. I do not remember all my tries, but I can recall most of them I think. I believe that the try I scored at the World Cup left a good impression with everybody. For me, in front of all those people, showing them the attractiveness of rugby was a valuable experience. That was a really important try for me. But maybe it was the try I scored against Wales in 1999 that has left the biggest impression in my memory.'

BELOW May 2006, Hanazono Stadium. Daisuke Ohata sweeps past Zurab Mchedlishvili of Georgia and David Campese's Test try-scoring record.

The Quest for 'Bill'
Knuckles, the Wallabies and RWC 2007

by RAECHELLE EDWARDS

'Connolly's experience in France will give him inside knowledge that is sure to assist the Wallabies in their World Cup preparation.'

'Fractions win you games.' And new Wallabies coach John Connolly knows from experience that sometimes there's not much between winning and losing. He also understands that to win a World Cup, you really need to have a little bit of luck on your side. Australia have twice claimed the Webb Ellis Cup (which they nickname 'Bill'), but only just. 'When Australia won the World Cup in '99 we got through a semi-final on the back of a Stephen Larkham field goal [dropped goal],' Connolly noted.

And when the Wallabies were victorious in 1991, the team almost missed out on a place in the semi-final. It took 'a bit of inspiration from Michael Lynagh in the last 30 seconds' of the quarter-final against Ireland at Lansdowne Road to secure the spot. Australia just missed out on a home victory in 2003 when Johnny Wilkinson kicked a field goal in extra time.

'There is a very fine line between it ... You need luck on your side and you have to play very well. One without the other and you're not going to make it,' Connolly said.

The Australian Rugby Union knew that the team was stale, having lost eight internationals in 2005. Leaving Eddie Jones at the helm was a significant risk to the Wallabies' chances of winning in 2007, so they appointed a former character of the Australian rugby scene to the top job.

'Knuckles', as Connolly is known, is a no-nonsense coach with an up-front style reminiscent of the amateur era. An 'ocker' Queenslander with a passion for punting on the horses and the dogs, he was an interesting choice and his personality couldn't be more different from the analytical Jones. Stephen Larkham says that whereas Jones tried to do everything, 'Knuckles is more laid back ... he stands back and keeps an eye on the bigger picture and makes sure the team is functioning as a whole.'

Larkham seems to have new-found passion with the fresh attitude and methods of the new coaching staff. 'There is an enthusiastic group of players on board at the moment. We've got some good coaches and everyone is enjoying training and all of the new things that they have brought in this year seem to be working for us,' Larkham said.

The veteran fly half knows what it takes to win the World Cup and thinks the Australian side has the capacity to triumph in 2007. 'You need to have a really good build-up, a really good team, a good ethos in the team and a team that's really tight together ... Knuckles has built a really strong team, everyone gets on really well with one another and everyone knows one another quite well and that's important going into a tournament because you are going to be under a lot of pressure and you need to know that you can rely on one another when it comes down to it.'

Connolly had an impressive record as Queensland coach between 1989 and 2000, winning the Super 6 Championship once, the Super 10 Championship twice, the Super 12 Minor Premiership twice and Super 12 Coach of the Year twice. During this period he offered himself as Wallaby coach three times and was rejected on each occasion. Two of those applicants who were successful, Bob Dwyer and Rod Macqueen, went on to coach Australia to World Cup wins. But in 1995 Connolly was furious that he was passed over for Greg Smith. In those more political days, the New South Wales delegates on the Australian Rugby Union board used their voting numbers to secure the role for Smith.

The day after he was deposed as coach of Queensland in 2000 Connolly was offered a new coaching contract, this time in France. Five days later he was in Paris coaching Max Guazzini's Stade Francais. Six weeks later his team beat Perpignan in the French Championship final. In his second year Connolly took Stade to the final of the European Cup, only to be defeated in the final seconds by Leicester. Connolly said it was one of the highest-quality rugby matches he had ever been involved in.

Connolly's experience in France will give him inside knowledge that is sure to assist the Wallabies in their World Cup preparation. 'The challenge will be adapting to the French way of life for the players, the food to some extent, the hotel rooms, the TV and all those things for players to feel comfortable for several weeks,' he said.

Connolly knows that the French side will be very hard to beat in the World Cup ('They are fantastic playing at home.'). He cites the other two strong northern hemisphere chances as England and Ireland. 'In the

PREVIOUS PAGE Wallabies coach John 'Knuckles' Connolly watches his squad in training in the build-up to the second Test against England in June 2006.

RIGHT Josh Valentine, on for George Gregan, makes a break from scrum half on his Wallaby debut in the first Test against England at Sydney in 2006.

southern hemisphere New Zealand are a wonderful team, wonderful players and South Africa are always a force because they play with so much force.'

Larkham sees the Wallabies' toughest competitors for rugby's greatest prize as 'France, New Zealand and South Africa. I think England has fallen down a peg or two and whilst Scotland and Ireland are performing well I just don't think they are the same calibre as New Zealand or France and South Africa are always dark horses come World Cup time.'

Connolly has an impressive coaching CV, moving on from Paris to three years in Britain. He first coached Swansea in Wales, then was appointed director of rugby at Bath. He worked closely with Michael Foley, who had played under Connolly in Queensland, and by the end of 2003 Bath had turned around, fuelled by a strong forward pack, and led the English premiership by nine points. In 2003-04, the club won 18 of 22 matches under Connolly, only to lose the championship final to London Wasps. That same year Connolly was awarded Coach of the Year. In 2004-05 Knuckles took the side to the final of the Powergen Cup.

Interestingly, Australia have only ever won the Webb Ellis Cup in the northern hemisphere. Connolly's experience in this part of the world was fundamental in his appointment as Wallabies coach. Now 55, Connolly says his age, experience and attitude are an asset. 'I think it is the pinnacle for any person to play for his country or coach his country. It is a tremendous honour and for me it has come at an interesting stage of life. I think the older you get, the more reflective you become

and you appreciate it more. You're not looking for another job or another gig anywhere, so you're there for the right reasons. Politics don't play a part in it.'

Having no loyalties to particular players has certainly shaken up the Australian side and given new players an opportunity to show their wares. This is a positive step forward for Australian rugby. Coming into the role, Connolly saw the team's greatest weakness as lack of depth. 'Since we've gone from Super 6 to Super 10 to Super 12 to Super 14, we used to play 6 Tests a year and now we play 12 or 13. The more games we play, the more we are exposed to injury. Building a strong base of players is our challenge. Looking towards the World Cup, it's about building a bit of depth.'

Connolly is currently focused on a short-term fix but says solving the depth problem longer term for Australian rugby is '… a work in progress. I don't know if we'll ever overcome it, only having four provinces. There has to be a very close association between the states and the national body.'

The Wallabies' critical challenge before the World Cup is finding the right scrum half and keeping Larkham injury-free. 'The key players are the 9 and 10, the playmakers. Nine and 10 must be on top of their game. I think we have some wonderful players in a lot of positions but number 10 behind Stephen Larkham is an issue.

'It is a concern, [Mat] Rogers has been trialled there but we need to make sure we have the support right.'

It is simple. If Larkham is injured and unavailable for the Wallabies' World Cup campaign, their chances of winning plummet. Larkham downplays the team's dependence on him, claiming that relying on any one player is potentially 'disastrous' and he is right. But Connolly's other options, Rogers, Matt Giteau, Sam Norton-Knight, Berrick Barnes and possibly even Kurtley Beale, who will be fresh out of school at the time of the World Cup, lack the composure, vision and ability to direct that Larkham is blessed with.

Connolly knows that resting key players such as Larkham during the Super 14 is paramount to being competitive in France.

> **BELOW** The Wallaby front row, made up of debutants Rodney Blake and Tai McIsaac, plus Greg Holmes on the far side, prepares to engage England in the first Test at Sydney in June 2006, which Australia won 34-3.

Larkham is happy with this notion as he will be 33 at the time of the World Cup and after two years being plagued by injury he says, 'it's just around the corner until everything gives up'.

'The northern hemisphere is in a far better position for this than we are, finishing the season and being able to rest. We have the Super 14 and we have to be very conscious not to kill them during the Super 14,' Connolly said.

The Wallabies' coach is in negotiations with the states and the Australian Rugby Union to agree a strategy to mitigate the risk of injury and ensure players are reasonably fresh for the World Cup. 'In a World Cup year and with the Super 14 starting early, we can't expect them to play right through until October.' Knuckles will surely be sympathetic to the Super 14 coaches, as he once coached Queensland at that level and was protective of his players. But at that time the physical demands of the players were far from what they are now in the congested international rugby calendar.

The half-back position is contentious, with George Gregan, Sam Cordingley, Josh Valentine and young Josh Holmes all in the mix. Connolly is also keen to blood some new talent on the Wallabies' end-of-year tour. That trip will be crucial to getting selections for the World Cup right.

Larkham identifies some youngsters he sees as budding stars for Australia: 'Cameron Shepherd, Sam Norton-Knight and Matt Giteau ... he's still a young guy who can potentially be a star of the World Cup,' he said. 'We've got Josh Valentine in the squad ... he is a very skilful half back and I imagine in years to come he'll be quite instrumental in the Wallabies.

'In the forward pack they've picked a couple of front-rowers who are looking very promising, [Greg] Holmes and [Rodney] Blake look skilful and fit into the team very well and everyone's very happy to play with them. And I think the other player that I'd like to mention is Wycliff Palu ... so far with the Wallabies he's been quite devastating.'

Connolly and forwards coach Foley are also focusing on rebuilding the forward pack, particularly the scrum, just as they did at Bath. Connolly was well known in Australian rugby circles for playing a ten-man game. But he says that ensuring the team is competitive up front does not mean the Wallabies will revert to a forward-oriented game. 'The game has evolved. Coaches evolve as well,' Connolly commented.

Connolly's backs coach, Scott Johnson, is well known for his attacking style. He would not have accepted an offer to join Connolly's coaching staff if he thought the Wallabies were going to play boring ten-man rugby. Johnson spent four seasons as an assistant coach with Wales. His original thinking was a key ingredient in the Welsh team's development into a competitive side that won the Six Nations Championship in 2005 playing an expansive game.

Wales offered Johnson the head coaching role, but he decided to decline the offer and return to Australia and support Connolly in the Wallabies' World Cup preparations. 'I hope we will be a team that reflects the Australian culture of having a go,' Johnson said.

Larkham has been impressed with Johnson: 'He has been really good for the team ... so far he has kept it really simple and everyone really appreciates that. We are working on becoming more skilful as individuals and as a team as opposed to the past where we concentrated on set piece and specific lines to run. I think everyone is improving their skill base as a whole.'

The Wallabies and Wales are in the same pool in 2007. 'Playing at Cardiff gives them an advantage and the crowd will be very boisterous as we experienced in the '99 World Cup,' Larkham said. 'But I think we've got one benefit in that we've got Scott Johnson coaching us now and he certainly knows how the Welsh play and I think that they're not going to change their style too much because they've had so much success with their style of play over the last couple of years so I think they'll be the ones who are concerned going into that game because we've got Scott Johnson on board,' he continued.

Connolly says of Australia's chances in the World Cup, 'I think we can be very competitive.' So, how is he going to ensure they are genuine contenders? 'Keep working the way we are to develop the depth in the squad and expand the way we play to some extent. I think people overemphasise style, I think at the top level you want to do everything well.'

John Eales, who played in Connolly's side in Queensland, says that his strength as a coach is that he understands his players and how to get the best out of them. 'I try to work with the players to get a result. I am not a dominant coach, it's about a team approach,' Connolly explained.

Knuckles has a simple philosophy: 'Only one thing makes good coaches. Good players.'

Faces of the Future
the U19 and U21 World Championships by ALAN LORIMER

'The talk in France was for the IRB to merge the Under 19 and Under 21 championships into one competition at Under 20 level. That and other options have yet to be discussed fully ...'

Administratively it may have been used as a dry run for next year's World Cup, but the 2006 IRB Under 21 World Championship, staged in the stunningly beautiful Auvergne region, ultimately provided France with the perfect stage on which to demonstrate future strength in global rugby.

In the event Les Bleus grabbed their chance, downing the defending champions, South Africa, with a tireless display of tightly controlled rugby to win the final at the Stade Marcel Michelin. In the final, France, inspiringly captained by lock Loic Jacquet, of whom more in future years, revealed their own Johnny Wilkinson – *Monsieur le boot* Lionel Beauxis. The 21-year-old Beauxis, who represented France A when he was 19, turned in a prodigious performance, kicking six penalty goals and two drops to score all the French points in the Tricolores' 24-13 win over the Baby Boks.

It wasn't a one-man operation, however. France showed that they have a battalion of frightenly square-shaped props ready to step up to senior level and skill behind the scrum in the shape of full back Maxime Medard and wing Florian Denos. The two sides had met in the pool stages, from which match South Africa emerged winners in a close contest. But France managed to secure the all-important bonus point to win a place in the semi-finals and a clash with the Wallabies.

The third/fourth play-off was contested by Australia and New Zealand, two sides who had looked likely finalists during the earlier stages of the tournament but who in the crucial semi-finals were unable to deliver. Such play-offs are usually seen as a Cinderella prelude to the main fare on finals day, but on this occasion the match proved to be more main course than entree. Both camps had agreed to play an open game and in the event the public were rewarded with a try-fest that resulted in a 39-36 win for New Zealand. It was perhaps a disappointing end for Australia who in scything through the pool rounds had confirmed the view that Wallaby rugby is in much better shape now.

Numbers are not huge in Australia and therefore, in contrast to the likes of New Zealand and South Africa, what you see in an Under 21 side is what you'll see at senior level in a couple or so years. Look out for centre Anthony Faingaa, outside half Christian Lealiifano, and scrum half Josh Holmes, all of whom played in the Under 19 championship two months earlier, but who looked more than comfortable in an older age grade. From the New Zealand squad one player certain to advance is lock/flanker Michael Paterson, but keep an eye out for centre Stephen Brett and wing James Somerset.

Of the home unions it was England who finished on top of the heap, the Six Nations champions winning four of their five games but being unable to claim a place among the top four. Their only defeat was against New Zealand, and therein lay a telling contrast of styles. England, reliant on a monstrously large pack, ultimately could not cope with the stylish and quick back play of the junior All Blacks and paid the price.

But age-grade rugby is all about development, and England will be pleased with the likes of scrum half Ben Foden, No. 8 Jordan Crane, centre Toby Flood and prop Dave Wilson.

One place behind England were Ireland who can regard the championship as a success. Seeded ninth going into the tournament and having had a difficult Six Nations campaign, Ireland became stronger through the rounds, to finish in sixth position with fine performances from centre Darren Cave and outside half Kieran Hallet.

LEFT France skipper Loic Jacquet on the charge as his side beat South Africa 24-13 in the final to win the Under 21 title.

Wales, missing far too many of their Six Nations squad, were never going to be a force in this tournament, but they showed immense character in their final pool match against Argentina, salvaging a losers' bonus point with a last-minute score. Elsewhere, sixth seeds Scotland finished in a lowly tenth position after going down 19-21 to Fiji in their final match at Thiers. The Scots were looking in control when they led 19-14 in the second half, but then an electrical storm and a white-out of hailstones changed everything. The referee opted not to stop the match and when Fiji kicked high into the hail-filled heavens the ball was lost from view. But when it returned to earth it bounced kindly to give Fiji the winning score. Scotland, however, can look to players like scrum half Greig Laidlaw, nephew of the great Roy, centre Ben Cairns and flanker Ross Rennie to add to their stock of professional footballers.

Fiji rightly celebrated a ninth-place finish after playing some hugely entertaining rugby that gave one the suspicion that their XV consisted of two sevens teams plus a tight-head prop. More seriously, the input of IRB coaching appears to have given the Fijians a more structured game that bodes well for the future.

Italy, meanwhile, struggled. Yet they were still better than the whipping boys, Georgia, whose inclusion in the championship had to be questioned, so far off the pace were they.

Two months earlier, Dubai, already synonymous with international sevens, expanded its global rugby links with the staging of the 2006 IRB Under 19 World Championship, providing the 24 participating teams with three weeks of sun, sand and sizzlingly hot sport.

In the high temperatures of the UAE it was Australia who emerged as worthy winners, defeating New Zealand in a gripping final at the Dubai Exiles ground. Two years ago in Durban, Australia disappointed hugely, going down to Wales in the fifth/sixth play-off. Last year, however, at the same South African venue the Wallabies gave notice that they were serious about the Under 19 World Championship and were unlucky not to make the final after losing to New Zealand in a penalty shoot-out.

The young Wallabies, with five of their players contracted to Super 14 squads, among them twins Saia and Anthony Faingaa of the Brumbies and influential scrum half Josh Holmes of the Waratahs, were always going to be a threat in the 2006 tournament. In the event it proved to be the case as Australia ran in 12 tries against a stunned Scotland side to win their opening tie 78-3 before overwhelming Romania by an even greater margin.

The one slip-up was against New Zealand in the final pool match, but the structure of the championship ensures that each team has two bites at the cherry. In the semi-final Australia, despite losing Super 14 wing Brett Stapleton as the result of a highly dangerous spear tackle, triumphed over France to book their place in the final against New Zealand.

New Zealand, too, had looked hungry for success, and their attractive style of play, in which full back-cum-stand-off Colin Slade, centres Male Sa'u and Tim Bateman, and skipper Victor Vito in the back row stood out as star material, won them admirers. An eventually comfortable win over Wales, a massive victory against Japan and then success against Australia left the Baby Blacks at the top of the pile after the pool stages and facing England in the semi-finals.

England, powerful up front but unable to match the Baby Blacks' inventive back play, were no match for New Zealand and once again were left contesting the third/fourth play-off, this time against a French side that had shocked the tournament by defeating defending champions South Africa 42-3 in the opening round.

But when Ireland ran the Tricolores close in their second-round match at the Exiles, France were exposed and their championship credentials became questionable. Indiscipline in the semi-final against Australia and the resultant suspensions knocked France off their stride, and it was not surprising that they lost to England in the final round.

Arguably the most successful side in the A division was Ireland. Seeded ninth going into the Dubai tournament and having lost all of their Six Nations matches, Ireland finished fifth overall and were one of only three teams to win four out of their five matches. Ireland's championship began with a first-round upset, a 17-16 defeat of England. Ireland then lost to France in a close game in which they were desperately unlucky not to collect a bonus point.

But thereafter the wheels went back on the wagon as Ireland chalked up wins against Samoa and Argentina before causing yet another upset by defeating Six Nations champions Wales through the reliable goal-kicking of Brian Collins, the tactical nous of scrum half David Drake and the inspired leadership of flanker David Pollock. For Wales, Dubai was undoubtedly a bitter disappointment after their Six Nations success. Whereas Ireland were able to improve massively at the championship Wales appeared stuck on their Six Nations plateau.

Occupying seventh position were Argentina, who had a star of the future in stand-off Ignacio Mieres but who were unable to settle on a style of game for the narrower pitches of Sharjah.

Undoubtedly the shock of the tournament was the demise of South Africa after slipping from first to eighth in the space of a year. The insider chat was that this was just one of those years when South Africa did not have the quality players of past seasons, but the truth probably lies in the fact that the other leading nations have simply become better.

For teams that fall into the positions from 9 to 12 at the end of the pool rounds, the fear of relegation becomes an issue. It looked as though Scotland might be heading for the trapdoor after big defeats against Australia and Wales, but then the Scots found their form to win their last three games, thus ensuring continued tenure in the top division.

For Scotland, however, there was a warning (not least from onlooking national coach Frank Hadden) that unless domestic competition becomes more intense and overall physical conditioning is improved then Scotland will not survive in the A division. Chasing Scotland for ninth spot were the Samoans. Newly promoted, the Pacific islanders caused problems for Ireland and Argentina but were ultimately let down by their indiscipline. That left Japan and Romania fighting out the relegation battle.

In the B division there was really only one team. Fiji were simply a revelation and proof that the IRB's investment in Pacific island rugby development has paid off handsomely. Moreover, Fiji provided huge entertainment whenever they took the field, with a reinvention of the handling game that produced some great tries, their coach Josua Toakula admitting that sevens rugby was a huge influence on their style of play.

Fiji backed their handling skills in what was always going to be a tough final against Pacific island rivals Tonga and in the event the Fijians triumphed in glorious fashion.

Elsewhere in the B division, Italy revealed much-improved back play, Canada emerged as a potential powerhouse (although they need better skills behind the scrum), Uruguay maintained the South American challenge and there was enterprise from Chile, Korea, USA and Taiwan.

As for Dubai, the venue was generally deemed a success, despite the challenging problems created by high temperatures that restricted both training and competition to the evening. Overall the standard of rugby in the tournament maintained its upward trend, but that was hardly surprising given the number of players attached to professional clubs.

As for the future of global age-grade tournaments, the next Under 19 championship is scheduled for Belfast in 2007, while the next at Under 21 level is due to take place in Wales a year later. Thereafter serious decisions have to be made. The talk in France was for the IRB to merge the Under 19 and Under 21 championships into one competition at Under 20 level. That and other options have yet to be discussed fully, but as world rugby moves on, what seems certain is that a new format will emerge.

Summer Tours 2006
England in Australia

by MICK CLEARY

'There was little of good that could be drawn from the experience, a verdict that is all the more troubling given that there was a half-full feel after ... the first Test in Sydney.'

Even though other Englishmen before them have travelled to Australia for a spot of hard labour, Andy Robinson's men might have imagined that the punishment inflicted by the locals would not have been quite so severe. At least, though, they got to return home after a fortnight's suffering.

There was little of good that could be drawn from the experience, a verdict that is all the more troubling given that there was a half-full feel after England's display in the first Test in Sydney. True, England did suffer their third-heaviest ever defeat to Australia, losing 34-3, but at least there was a sense of ambition and devil about their play. Two late Wallaby tries, from wing Mark Gerrard and humungous prop Rodney 'Rodzilla' Blake, had given an unsympathetic spin to the scoreboard.

False dawns all round. England were truly dreadful six days later in Melbourne, misshapen and mis-selected. All the promise of the previous weekend had completely evaporated. Half-full had become almost entirely empty in one dispiriting gulp.

How so? Simple. England had set out to Australia with the express intention of finding a new way forward, of laying down markers for the future under their new coaching team of Brian Ashton (attack), John Wells (forwards) and Mike Ford (defence). England were also keen to really test the mettle of certain players to see if they could cut it in the rough 'n' tumble world of international rugby. Catching the eye at club level is one thing; doing the same among the big boys quite another.

So, Magnus Lund, what are you made of? You may have ruled the open-side roost in the Premiership, but how good are you without your thickset, rampaging back-row mates at Sale – Jason White and Sebastien Chabal? Likewise Olly Barkley, a player whose reputation soared during his enforced absence through injury from the Six Nations Championship. Barkley was to be the shrewd, clever orchestrator, either at fly half or inside centre. Indeed, a centre combination of Barkley alongside Newcastle's Mathew Tait had World Cup possibilities written all over it. Tait – another one to find out about. Tom Varndell – ditto. And what did we get in terms of conclusive evidence? Absolutely nothing.

Lund was played out of position in the first Test, mixing and matching with Lewis Moody on the open side. He was dropped to the bench for the second Test, then passed over for Bath's Michael Lipman when Moody pulled out on the morning of the game. Lund did get a bit of a run in the second half before retiring injured. Verdict: no idea. Do the England selectors rate Lund or not? The case for bringing in Lipman ahead of him was that they needed to have an over-the-ball dog on the open side to counter George Smith. How did they know for sure that Lund was not up to the job? Play him and find out once and for all was the only sensible thing to do. England did not do the sensible thing.

The same was true of Tait. There were a couple of promising shimmies in the first Test, a mere glimpse if truth be told of what latent goodies there might be in those boots. Others showed more sustained form in that Sydney game and Tait himself was frustrated that he did not get his hands on the ball more often. Still, there was always next week …

Now, left wing is not the worst position to play. Jonah Lomu didn't do too badly out of wearing the number 11 shirt. He was big, he was bold and he knew that every black shirt on the field was trying to move the ball to him while every single bloke in the opposition was praying that he didn't get it. Tait is no Lomu. Never mind that. We'll never find out if Tait is an outside centre if he's picked on the wing. Andy Robinson was quick to point out that it was all part of a cunning plan and that Tait would actually appear in the outside channel in attack, trading places with Newcastle team-mate Jamie Noon in defence. Big deal. It didn't really come to pass. Why didn't the selectors, particularly after their crass handling of Tait the previous year, let the youngster find his feet in his customary position? We still don't know if Tait is up to scratch. We think he is but we don't know that he is. Chance missed.

FACING PAGE Mathew Tait, playing not at centre in this game but on the left wing, is flattened by the Wallaby defence, with Rocky Elsom and Daniel Vickerman to the fore, as England go down 43-18 in the second Test at Melbourne.

Barkley had a run at fly half in Sydney, even though he has played most of his club rugby at inside centre. He then found himself out on his backside as England opted for the more direct but more predictable talents of Andy Goode. The spoke in the selectorial wheel was Mike Catt, the born-again London Irish player who has found his form since leaving Bath.

Catt had had a terrific Premiership season and clearly had something to offer. Yet Catt, 35 in September, is no more than a wild outside punt for the World Cup side. Another year older, how will that body be holding up for the full-frontal assault course that is a World Cup? So, what was his true purpose in Australia? Was he there to shore things up in midfield or was he there as a genuine contender? If the latter, then fine. But say so. Catt did pretty well across the two Tests, although the infuriating tendency of the back line to shunt the ball across the field, landing Tom Varndell with a whole heap of dreadlocked trouble in the shape of Lote Tuqiri was none too clever.

Catt was there to direct such operations with more subtlety and variation. When pressed as to why Barkley had not been given a start at inside centre, Robinson replied that it was felt that with so many inexperienced players around, the team needed the wise head of Catt. How on earth are players going to become seasoned international performers if they are not trusted with playing Test rugby? If Tait and Varndell, along with scrum half Peter Richards, do need mollycoddling then they shouldn't be there in the first place. Barkley, too, is no spotty teenager. He has played Premiership rugby for five years.

It was all rather depressing. Nothing learnt, nothing gained. England might care to point to the form of lock forwards Ben Kay and Chris Jones, as well as the invigorating full debut of hooker George Chuter, begging the question, though, of why the second-row combo was not on duty in the first Test.

Robinson always knew that the two-Test trip was going to be a tough one, another burden in what had been a difficult year. He could have handled it better. The decision to leave behind 18 front-line players was the correct one, even though many of us are in a state of despair at the ever-diminishing value of Test rugby. Every coach on the planet now bleats on about shuffling their resources in the interests of the 2007 World Cup. Let's play the 2007 Rugby World Cup when it's September 2007 and not before. The International Rugby Board has a duty to preserve the integrity of Test match rugby and should apply sanctions if it believes that countries are deliberately fielding understrength teams.

There is too much Test rugby played. The revamped, bloated Tri-Nations tournament is proof of that. Robinson took a predictable swipe at the congested, muddled domestic fixture list in England as one of the prime difficulties he had in 'delivering world-class performers' to the international stage. Well, after leaving Australia Robinson could look forward to 14 Tests prior to the start of the World Cup. Coupled with training days, that means Robinson will have the players at his disposal for at least four months. That's not a bad slice of action.

We all know that the schedule needs an overhaul. We know that the domestic season is a pig's ear. But it's not so bad that it can't be worked through. England's problems lie closer to home. It's to be hoped that they will be addressed and rectified once the new coaching team beds down.

For the record, Australia, with a reconstituted rookie front row with only three caps between them, were strong enough to withstand anything that England could hurl their way in the first Test. England were unlucky when the television match official ruled against a first-half score by Iain Balshaw, the try saved by a magnificent clawback intervention by George Gregan. They eventually ran out of steam and ideas. Australia, with eight losses from their previous nine games, were clearly the better side, tries coming from Chris Latham followed by the late brace from Gerrard and Blake.

The second Test was a chaotic mess of a match with uncontested scrums throughout the second half following injuries to Graham Rowntree and Julian White. Australia ran in six tries, from Gerrard (two), George Smith, Tuqiri, Mark Chisholm and Stephen Larkham. England replied with tries from Chuter and Varndell in a final score of 43-18. They were no consolation whatsoever.

Scotland in South Africa

by ALAN LORIMER

'Scotland may have lost the series, but they showed in the second Test that they could front up in the forward battle and moreover defend tenaciously.'

There had been a genuine feeling of expectation in the run-up to Scotland's two-Test tour of South Africa in June, but in the event the Scots were unable to reproduce their recent form, ultimately paying the price with a 2-0 series defeat.

Of course it can be argued that the results of summer tours are of little consequence beyond the immediate psychological lift obtained. What Scotland coach Frank Hadden had hoped to achieve was a consolidation of team-building begun in November 2005 and continued successfully through the 2006 Six Nations Championship.

Hadden also took the chance to widen his squad with the recall of flanker Donnie Macfadyen, the inclusion of pacy scrum half Sam Pinder for the injured Chris Cusiter and the selection of Borders flanker Kelly Brown, a player who could yet make a mark in the 2007 Rugby World Cup.

Macfadyen, a genuine open-sider, was given an immediate chance to prove himself after being

selected to play in the first Test at Durban. But in the event there was little for him to scavenge as Scotland were put on the back foot by a Springbok pack that bullied the visitors into a submissive role both at the set piece and at the contact area.

The 36-16 final scoreline was not surprising, the Scots' points coming from three penalties by Chris Paterson, who also converted a late try by substitute Simon Webster. For South Africa Schalk Burger, Breyton Paulse, Andre Snyman and Percy Montgomery all crossed, the latter accounting for the remaining points with his accurate boot.

A week later the Test arena was Port Elizabeth, but sadly for the Scots the outcome was the same, if not the manner of defeat. Scotland could feel slightly cheated, having had two 'scores' disallowed. But these two decisions aside, the tourists proved to be more physical and competitive than in the first Test, their blanket defence being far more evident as they shut down the Springboks in attack and disrupted their set-piece play.

In the end Scotland won the try count 2-1, achieving touchdowns from Webster and Macfadyen against that of Fourie du Preez for South Africa. But with Montgomery kicking seven penalties and Jaco van der Westhuyzen adding another, the Boks emerged winners 29-15. Hadden was understandably cautious in making any criticism of the referee over the two disallowed tries but could not resist commenting: 'Who would have thought the number two side in the world would need a couple of dodgy decisions to beat us on their own turf. We played well enough to win – but they had all the luck that was going.'

Scotland may have lost the series, but they showed in the second Test that they could front up in the forward battle and moreover defend tenaciously. There remain problems behind the scrum, but with Gordon Ross moving ahead for the outside-half position and Simon Webster making an impact in both Tests, there are some encouraging signs for Scotland.

LEFT Flanker Kelly Brown (right) and scrum half Sam Pinder get to grips with Springbok replacement prop C.J. van der Linde in the second Test at Port Elizabeth, which South Africa won 29-15.

Wales in Argentina

by GRAHAM CLUTTON

> "'I really do hope we are competitive during the period before next year's World Cup. We have got to have at least two people in every position competing for the jersey.'"

With an entire side, and more, having been ruled out of the June tour to Argentina, Wales, under the guidance of new coach Gareth Jenkins, suffered successive Test match defeats at the hands of the Pumas. However, when the dust settled on the young Dragons' 14-day excursion to Patagonia and Buenos Aires, Jenkins and his young coaching team of Nigel Davies, Neil Jenkins, Robin McBryde and Rowland Phillips were understandably delighted with the way in which their young charges had responded to the physical examination.

Admittedly, back-to-back defeats and a lengthy ban for the young Ospreys lock Ian Evans, for charging, provided a sobering balance. But in heading south with such a young squad, and one with precious little experience at international level, Jenkins was able to take a close look at those fringe players who will be challenging for World Cup shirts when they are handed out in France next year.

Although Wales lost the Test matches 27-25 (Patagonia) and 45-27 (Buenos Aires), there was plenty to enthuse over. Under 21 internationals James Hook and Alun Wyn Jones were, perhaps, the two individuals who stood out whilst the continuing form of other young players like Michael Phillips, Huw Bennett and Lee Byrne did not go unnoticed.

'Of course it was disappointing not to have won a game out there, but with so many players ruled out because of injury or the necessity for rest, we had to lower our expectation,' said Jenkins. 'Having said that, there were plenty of youngsters who benefited from that and as far as I am concerned, it can only hold us in good stead.

'In the first Test, we probably caught them a little cold and maybe, in the end, we could have won it. I was delighted with the way we played and the way we stood up to the physical challenge.

'The second game was a little different. They had enjoyed a further week together and I think that showed. We were soundly beaten although we can take something from that match too.'

But with Wales in a position to welcome back from injury so many of last year's Lions, Jenkins

RIGHT Matthew Watkins runs into heavy Argentine traffic as Alun Wyn Jones (left) and Duncan Jones provide support.

is understandably confident that better times lie ahead. Dwayne Peel, Brent Cockbain, Ryan Jones, Gavin Henson, Gethin Jenkins, Stephen Jones and Gareth Thomas were amongst the deep pool of players missing, and Jenkins called on the nation to take that into consideration before heaping too much criticism on the short excursion.

He said, 'You cannot ignore the fact that so many of our leading players were not there. Many of them have won a Six Nations Championship and have been through the emotion of a Lions tour. They have felt those experiences.

'Some of them are the best players in Britain and Ireland in their positions and they are available to us in the autumn, which is great news.'

For Henson, who is waiting in the wings after deciding to stay at home to concentrate on his fitness, Jenkins had a special word: 'Gavin's challenge is to get a real base of fitness. He feels his game depends on it and the off-season has provided him with a great opportunity to do just that.

'His region, the Ospreys, want him to have an injury-free period, and we agreed with them.'

In Argentina, Wales unearthed a potential rival to Henson for the number 12 jersey next season in the shape of Hook. The 20-year-old, a training partner of Henson at the Ospreys, shone during a debut-making, try-scoring appearance against Argentina and looks every bit a player capable of surviving and subsequently performing on the highest stage. He was a revelation after coming on

RIGHT Ian Evans heads for the Argentine line to score during the first Test at Puerto Madryn.

BELOW Federico Todeschini (left) and Gonzalo Longo put their bodies on the line as Mike Phillips hacks on in the first Test.

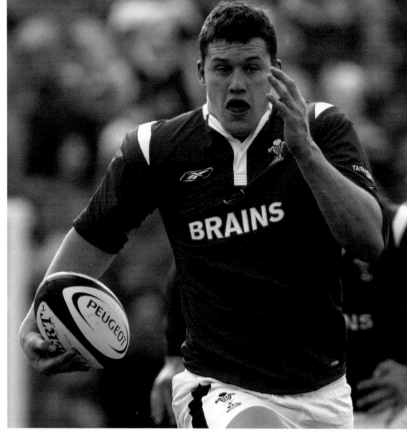

as a replacement in the first Test and was picked to start in the second. Hook showed great mental strength in bouncing back from a charge-down that led to an Argentine try, missed kicks and a sin-binning for a high tackle by making a classic break to create a try during a late Welsh revival.

'There were at least half a dozen players on the tour who could end up figuring in the 30 players to go to the World Cup next year,' said Jenkins. 'And I would say there were maybe ten players who will be playing at the World Cup after next. I certainly think we will see, come the autumn and the Six Nations, the benefits of the decisions made this summer.

'The autumn is the key to implementing our strategies with the complete group of players we hope to have. I really do hope we are competitive during the period before next year's World Cup. We have got to have at least two people in every position competing for the jersey.

'The national team is really about one thing and that doesn't change. It's called winning.'

Jenkins was delighted with the contribution of caretaker coaches Rowland Phillips (defence), Neil Jenkins (kicking) and Robin McBryde (forwards) in Argentina and said, 'I was very pleased with the way we, as a group, gelled and worked together.

'Rowland was very positive, while Neil demonstrated his qualities as a rugby mind and as a specific technical assistant in developing individual players.

'And Robin was a real quality boy to work with. What he has got is respect with the players having a fantastic reaction to him.

'All in all I am far from downbeat with the tour and I look forward to watching these players come through during the domestic season and challenging, once again, for places in next year's World Cup squad.'

Ireland Down Under

by SEAN DIFFLEY

'No. 8 Denis Leamy was the outstanding Irish forward in all three Tests and that young man seems destined for a star future. Neil Best, too, was a discovery at flank forward ...'

Although Ireland lost all three Tests – two to the All Blacks, in Hamilton and Auckland, and the third to the Wallabies in Perth – there were occasions in all three when an Irish win was definitely on the cards. But as the newspaper headlines aptly put it: 'Ireland earn respect, but run out of steam', and 'Another one gets away in the finish'. There was some criticism at what was perceived as coach Eddie O'Sullivan's sparse use of his bench, but the counter to that argument was that the replacements were hardly all that strong. Even though Ireland took the Triple Crown in the Six Nations, Munster won the Heineken Cup and Ulster, Leinster and Munster finished in that order at the top of the Celtic League, the reality is that a small playing population means comparatively few of international class.

There was no doubt but the long home season meant that the touring Irish looked a tired side in each of the three Tests, even though O'Sullivan tended to dismiss that as an excuse. Perhaps those end-of-season tours are inadvisable and place far too much strain on overplayed teams, but the economic facts of the professional game are that the finance generated is a basic requirement.

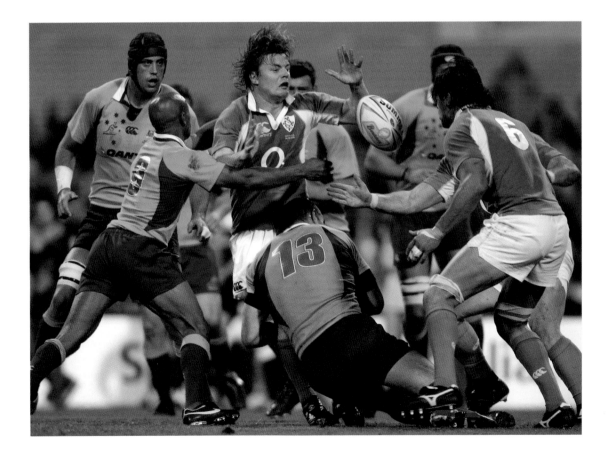

Ireland lost the first tilt at the All Blacks 34-23 and the second 27-17. On both occasions Ireland's hopes were high, but their last scores came midway through the respective second halves. The greater physical bulk of the New Zealand forwards reduced the Irish scrum to rearwards crawling, and in the last 20 minutes of the two Tests the All Blacks registered an aggregate of 29 points to nil points for the Irish. Against the Australians in Perth, Ireland led 15-11 with 20 minutes left, but then succumbed to a similar disaster in the final stages, losing 37-15. And a further disquieting feature was the Irish line out. It had won the battle with the All Blacks, but Paul O'Connell and Donncha O'Callaghan were outplayed in that department in Perth.

The positives from the three-Test tour to the toughest part of the rugby world? No. 8 Denis Leamy was the outstanding Irish forward in all three Tests and that young man seems destined for a star future. Neil Best, too, was a discovery at flank forward, and those two with David Wallace did more than was expected of them – one very un-Irish element the trio introduced in Perth was the number of turnovers they managed against the Wallabies, of all people.

The Irish backs were, frankly, disappointing. Suggestions that the rear division was one of the best in world rugby were certainly not borne out. Brian O'Driscoll scored one great try against the All Blacks in the first Test and in all three was a notable defender. But generally the backs were outplayed by their opposite numbers. Much of that, of course, was caused by slow ball from the forwards under that intense physical pressure.

But the basic flaw? Relying on the same 15 or 16 for all the Tests. As Aussie coach John Connolly pointed out: 'You need a very strong bench and rugby is a 28-man squad now.'

FACING PAGE Brian O'Driscoll attracts plenty of attention against Australia at Perth.

RIGHT Denis Leamy snaffles line-out ball for Ireland against New Zealand at Hamilton.

Churchill Cup

by HUGH GODWIN

'And, whatever the figures say, any gathering of disparate rugby folk is likely to leave the observer with positive memories, and this one was no different.'

ABOVE New Zealand Maori with the Cup after their 52-17 win over Scotland A in the final.

FACING PAGE The Saxons' Delon Armitage catches up with Scotland A's Calum MacRae in wet conditions in Toronto.

The RFU took a leap of faith in 2003 when they signed up to an initial five-year deal to participate in and help promote the Churchill Cup. For the fourth occasion of the annual tournament in Canada and the USA in June 2006 there was a first title sponsor in Barclays and an increase in the number of teams from four to six. Purely in terms of attendances at the nine matches (each of which was broadcast live to the UK by BSkyB), the event might be considered still more acorn than mighty oak. Undoubtedly, though, the notion of developing rugby in North America through competition – a principle dear to the International Rugby Board's heart – is being well served.

The bean counters have much to mull over. To use the vernacular, the Churchill Cup's penetration of the North American market is not yet what the organisers would like. One wonders if it was wise to have such huge distances between the venues – from Toronto

and Ottawa in the east to Santa Clara, California, in the west. When the six teams mustered for finals day at Edmonton's 55,000-seat Commonwealth Stadium, just short of 8000 people turned up to watch. The location of next year's matches is under review, not least because it will be the USA's turn to host the finals.

But the RFU are in for the long haul until 2013 at least under their strategic plan, having placed £1 million in the pot in the form of a loan, while the IRB chipped in with £200,000 to fund the participation of Ireland A and Scotland A for the first time. And, whatever the figures say, any gathering of disparate rugby folk is likely to leave the observer with positive memories, and this one was no different. It was a pleasure to be there.

The Cup was won by the New Zealand Maori – they had prevailed, too, on their previous appearance in 2004 – with some high-quality rugby in a 52-17 trouncing of Scotland A in Edmonton. Quite a tribute to the New Zealanders' strength in depth, given there were senior and junior All Black teams, not to mention the Under 21s, doing the rounds elsewhere in the world.

England's role as patron was no guarantee of success on the field. England A, the title holders, arrived with an ambivalently received new soubriquet – the Saxons – and two coaches in Jon Callard and Simon Hardy who had taken charge at the eleventh hour after the reshuffle of Andy Robinson's senior staff. A familiar refrain was the lack of preparation time, although the Saxons' scrum and line out knitted together very quickly and effectively. The developmental aspect to the trip dictated that players in specialist positions were rotated. For instance, a different scrum half started each match – though the strong performances of Paul Hodgson, Richard Wigglesworth and Clive Stuart-Smith debunked the accepted wisdom that England were short of cover in the number 9 jersey.

Nevertheless the Saxons' baptism misfired when they lost their first Pool A match to Scotland A at York University in Toronto. The Scots resisted the temptation to call themselves the Picts. They did adapt better to the rainy conditions, though, winning 13-7 to the delight of their coach, Steve Bates, ironically a former England A (and England) scrum half. Quick rucking by the back row and a

defiant last-ditch goal-line stand were the highlights. Shades of old Calcutta Cup triumphs, although England had a perfectly good try by the Saracens flanker David Seymour ruled out – no television match officials here – and another tossed away on the wing by Chris Bell when he dived early for the line and the ball bounced from his grasp.

That left Scotland A needing to beat Canada

four days later to top Pool A and reach the final. Twin Elm Rugby Park, a few miles outside Ottawa, was the venue; the home club ground to the great Canadian forward Al Charron, who played in four World Cups before retiring in 2003. Charron was one of 13 local players from down the ages who received their Test caps at half-time. That ceremony and a try by Canada's James Pritchard were acclaimed warmly by a crowd of around 5000. But Scotland had started the more assuredly, with tries by two of their full Test caps, Nikki Walker and Simon Danielli. And they finished off a 15-10 win with the only score of the second half, a dropped goal by fly half Phil Godman.

Meanwhile, half a continent away in California, Ireland A took time off to serenade 37,000 baseball fans with 'Take me out to the ball game' at the San Francisco Giants' 'Irish Heritage' night. Back with the rugby, the Irish kicked off Pool B by defeating the USA by 28 points to 13. Then the Maori, captained by Jono Gibbes, ran in 12 tries against the USA to win 74-6; a chastening experience for the experimental Eagles. In the deciding match the Maori were put out of their stride to a certain extent by Ireland's aggressive forwards, but Liam Messam – a dynamic partner in crime to Gibbes in the back row – got one of the New Zealanders' four tries in a 27-6 win.

Already aware that the cup final was beyond them, England Saxons finished Pool A in welcome sunshine at York University with a 41-11 defeat of Canada, a few of whose leading lights were absent with their French clubs. The English handling was much better than it had been against the Scots, and the back three and back row were prominent. Two tries went to the London Irish full back Delon Armitage, and one each to Richard Haughton, Kai Horstmann, Bell and Ben Woods. Few can deny that at every level England have pace to burn in the wide channels. We wait to see if the players and coaches concerned know how best to harness it.

Edmonton was in the grip of ice hockey fever with the home-town Oilers engaged in the Stanley Cup final. Meanwhile, England Saxons had third place in the Churchill Cup to shoot for and they led Ireland A 22-13 after 47 minutes through tries by the Worcester No. 8 Horstmann, Wasps wing Ayoola Erinle and centre Sam Vesty of Leicester. The Irish fought back to nick a one-point lead with tries by forwards Matt McCullough and John Fogarty, but England captain for the day Ben Johnston went over in the last minute of normal time to make it 27-23. By then the Saxons had their tour skipper David Barnes in the sin bin for pulling down Ireland's driving maul, and flanker Andy Beattie was soon to follow for a similar offence. A third yellow card went to London Irish's hooker David Paice for fighting, and it coincided with the Irish forcing their replacement prop Ronan McCormack over for the winning try, converted by Paddy Wallace for a final score of 30-27.

The neighbourly scrap over fifth place went the way of Canada, 33-18, with the 6ft 5ins wing Justin Mensah-Coker, one of the successes of the tournament, adding to his reputation with two smartly taken tries. The USA appeared mired in political infighting, with an interim coaching team of Peter Thorburn, a New Zealander, and Alan Solomons, a South African, in place after the resignation of Tom Billups. The short-term task for Thorburn and Solomons was to prepare to face a full-strength Canada in the North American zone of the Rugby World Cup qualifiers. Long term, the USA share with the Canadians the challenge of making the best of talent from far-flung locations dominated by the 'Big Four' sports: gridiron, baseball, basketball and ice hockey. Different aims but a common bond: that was the theme of the 2006 Churchill Cup.

Destination France
RWC 2007 Round-up

by CHRIS THAU

'So on 7 September 2007, France v Argentina will be the opening shot of RWC 2007 ... the third time the Pumas have featured in the opening match of an RWC tournament.'

For a short while in early 2006 the rugby headlines were stolen by the race between Japan, New Zealand and South Africa for the right to host RWC 2011. In the end, after a brilliant tactical campaign devised and implemented by NZRU chairman Jock Hobbs and CEO Chris Moller, New Zealand won the bid and with it the right to stage the seventh RWC tournament. With the decision on the host nation for RWC 2011 out of the way, the soccer World Cup briefly stole the limelight, but as soon as it was gone in turn, minds, and significantly resources, could safely be concentrated on the next global event, the biggest in the world next year, RWC 2007 in France.

Indeed, as the preparations for the sixth RWC gather momentum, the race for the coveted starting slots in the tournament is heating up. Over 150 matches have been played in the qualifying

RIGHT India and Kazakhstan fight it out in Mumbai in the second round of the Asian zone. The Kazakhs prevailed 36-22.

FACING PAGE Hong Kong on the attack against Sri Lanka at the Hong Kong Football Club in a match the hosts won 45-14.

rounds so far, involving nearly 100 nations in the five IRB regions: Europe, Pacific, Africa, Asia and Americas. By the end of the qualifying cycle next spring, the 20-strong line-up will be known.

Early in July, Argentina became the third nation to qualify for the finals, after Samoa and Fiji, when they defeated Uruguay 26-0 in tropical rain in Buenos Aires. It was harder than anyone expected, but then when Los Teros play Los Pumas, no prisoners are taken and the intensity of the encounter defies the odds and the lowly status of the Uruguayans. In the end, although the final result was never in doubt, it took a splendid effort from Worcester centre Miguel Avramovic, who scored two tries, and the metronomic precision with the boot of new fly half Federico Todeschini to subdue the lively Uruguayans and secure a satisfying, if not glamorous, win for the Pumas.

'Playing in a Rugby World Cup is the most important objective that you can achieve as a player and therefore we are extremely pleased to have qualified. It was a tough match and Uruguay were tough opposition, but I am pleased with the patience that we showed in difficult conditions to win the match,' said Argentina captain Agustin Pichot.

So on 7 September 2007, France v Argentina will be the opening shot of RWC 2007, a genuine treat for the connoisseur and the third time the Pumas have featured in the opening match of an RWC tournament.

'Playing in France will be an exciting experience for this team and will give us an opportunity to put right what were disappointing results in the last two tournaments and push to progress to the quarter-finals. I live in Paris, so I know exactly what to expect. It will be an incredible atmosphere and the French public will embrace the tournament and get behind their team. So for us it will be a great pleasure to open Rugby World Cup 2007, but also an extremely challenging game, but one which we are very much looking forward to,' added Pichot.

LEFT German wing Mustafa Gungor signs autographs after he contributed a try to his side's defeat of Belgium, which saw them top Pool B of Europe Round Three.

ABOVE LEFT Germany and Belgium pack down in Hanover.

The hopes of Los Teros for a place in the 2007 finals were kept alive after they defeated Chile 43-15 on 22 July in Montevideo. Uruguay take on the runners-up in the North American (NAWIRA) pool – either Canada or the US Eagles, who both ran up cricket scores (69-3 and 91-0 respectively) against brave Barbados, unexpected fellow-travellers at this level of the regional competition. The two North American teams have called all their professionals back from Europe for the crunch encounter in Newfoundland on 12 August, which will provide the second American qualifier for France, in Pool B alongside Australia, Wales and Fiji. The third Americas slot, in Pool A, together with England, South Africa and Samoa, will go to the winner of the Americas play-off between Uruguay and the loser in St John's. And even then, the loser of this match still has a chance of reaching France 2007 via the Repechage.

The long and protracted European qualifying process, which started in September 2004 in the Principality of Andorra, arguably the smallest IRB member, has entered the final stages involving the 'big' Continental boys: Italy, Romania, Georgia, Portugal and Russia. The meritocratic nature of the system has brought to the fore the likes of Moldova, Andorra, Belgium and Germany, until this season languishing in the lower divisions of the pyramidal European FIRA-AER league. Eventually a much-improved Germany, captained by Jens Schmidt and with their sole professional player, Robert Mohr of La Rochelle, returning to his home town of Hanover for the big match, prevailed 33-15 at the end of a bruising encounter against a young and committed Belgian team in April. They thus secured themselves a place against Spain in the European home-and-away play-offs.

The Spanish, on the other hand, cut short any Dutch hope of an upset, defeating the Netherlands 24-13 in Madrid. In the end the Spanish, coached by Englishman Gerard Glynn, used their home advantage to scrape through against a brave and committed German team with an aggregate score of 42-28. They won the crucial clash in Madrid 36-10, after losing the first one 18-6 in Heidelberg. In order to secure themselves a shot at one of the three European qualifying slots, the Spanish must first win a home-and-away play-off against the Czech Republic – fifth in the European Nations Cup – which may be beyond their current capabilities. The Russians, who finished fourth in the ENC after Portugal, take on Ukraine for the other place in the second European pool, likely to be dominated by Italy.

In Asia, Sri Lanka, under the legendary New Zealand coach George Simpkin, had hopes of reaching the final stages of the qualifying zone after a classy 30-0 win over the People's Republic of China. However, a resurgent Hong Kong defeated China, too – 23-7 in Shanghai – and also put the brave Sri Lankans to the sword 45-14 to deny them a place in the final round against Japan and Korea in November. The winner will end up in Pool C, together with New Zealand and Scotland and the top two European qualifiers, probably Italy and Romania.

Meanwhile, in the Pacific zone, Tonga easily won the play-off against Cook Islands to secure themselves a place in the first Repechage against the Asian runners-up, either Korea or Hong Kong. Finally, the African zone is well into an intriguing second round, with Uganda and Tunisia, in their respective pools, producing upsets in their first-leg matches against Cote d'Ivoire and Namibia. The Ugandans, who benefited from the unexpected bonus of having South African hero Chester Williams on their coaching team, beat Cote d'Ivoire 32-7 in Kampala, while the Tunisians demolished Namibia 24-7 in Tunis. The outcome of the match against Morocco in Kampala will most certainly decide the winner of Pool 2, Uganda having lost the away match in Casablanca 36-3. Similarly, the Namibians, who entertain Tunisia in Windhoek, are confident that they can reverse the score, having already beaten Kenya 84-12 in the first round of games. The winners of the two pools play one another home and away for the coveted African RWC slot in Pool D alongside the likes of France, Ireland and Argentina.

In the meantime, the preparations for the tournament have entered the final stages. All global sponsors are in place and the big TV contracts have been all but signed. The Organising Committee, led by dynamic former Racing Club de France and France utility forward Claude Atcher, has concluded deals with all hosting cities and venue operators in both France and the UK (Wales and Scotland). Finally, the RWC07 train (a huge promotional exercise across France supported by one of the sponsors, SNCF), which started its journey in the spring in the city of Le Havre, is making steady progress through the country and is scheduled to reach Paris, its final destination, in November, at the time of the centenary Test against the visiting All Blacks.

strength
&depth

With dedicated teams to tackle a wide range
of legal issues, we have the strength of
resource and depth of knowledge to provide
practical, commercial solutions.

T +44 (0)870 903 1000
www.wragge.com
Wragge & Co LLP is a
Limited Liability Partnership

HOME FRONT

When it comes to helping drivers after accidents, we're on the ball

"Why not take a look at how we could help you?"

If you've ever been involved in a road accident you'll know how inconvenient it can be...dealing with insurers, repairers, organising a courtesy car...not to mention claiming for any losses or compensation for injury. Even worse when the accident wasn't your fault!

Now there's a better way...simply call Helphire.

We're approved by the UK's leading insurers & can help by:

• Providing you with a like for like vehicle (if needed)
• Organising and funding your repairs
• Liaising with insurers & helping you claim for any losses

The car hire & repair bills are then passed to the insurance company of the driver that caused the accident so you don't have to pay.

You don't have to be a member – just call after an accident that you believe was not your fault and we'll do our best to help you.

Call **0500 224455** or visit **www.helphire.co.uk**

HELPHIRE ARE PROUD TO SUPPORT THE "WOODEN SPOON CHARITY"

Back in the Big Time
the Return of Harlequins

by CHRIS JONES

'Quins return keenly aware of the dangers that lurk in the Premiership. Get it wrong again and they will go down – a threat that looms over all but a couple of the top teams ...'

Harlequins, the most famous rugby club in the world, are back in the Guinness Premiership, having survived the ignominy of relegation and a financial loss of around £1 million. That is how much debt they ran up while out of the game's elite; given predictions in some quarters of three times that loss, it constitutes a victory of sorts, both on and off the pitch, for a team so many in the game still love to hate.

There weren't many tears shed for Quins when they went down after a narrow defeat to Sale at the Stoop. Since that black day, the squad has undergone reconstruction, the new Lexus Stand has opened raising capacity to 12,700, ex-England great Dean Richards has been installed as director of

rugby, London Broncos have come on board as Harlequins rugby league side playing in the same famous colours, and the ground has been renamed Twickenham Stoop. Patently, Quins were not treading water while out of the limelight!

Quins return keenly aware of the dangers that lurk in the Premiership. Get it wrong again and they will go down – a threat that looms over all but a couple of the top teams who have the playing strength to stay clear of the drop. It was Leeds who went down last season and immediately imploded, with players and management heading out of the exit door; but at least their financial backer is still in place to absorb the kind of loss Quins have dealt with over the past 12 months.

The Quins loss was half the financial burden the club was expecting to face, thanks to solid support from fans and sponsors, a £1.5 million parachute payment and cost-cutting actions. Mark Evans, the Quins chief executive, having had to deal with the problems caused by relegation, knows the task facing the club next season is even tougher.

He said: 'Our financial situation has transformed from four or five years ago because we have a real fan base and a stadium with a 12,700 capacity. We expect to have an operational break-even figure at the end of next season and we are a viable organisation.

'However, we know that the Premiership has, if that was possible, become even more competitive and you simply cannot find a team that doesn't have a number of quality players. The game is so much bigger and the gap between the top and bottom is small and who would have thought Sale, the top team this season, would have lost five games?

'We all know that Leeds were a hair's breadth away from beating Sale and Leicester. Northampton were, at the turn of the year, eleventh, and then suddenly pressing for Heineken Cup qualification. People make fewer mistakes in terms of recruitment and have more resources to play with. This is the most global of leagues in the sport and a real melting pot of ideas and talents.

'With the exception of say two or three clubs, I don't think anyone else can be certain of what is going to happen next season. The Premiership is that tight with very fine margins between winning and losing and that's why so many clubs had so much to play for in the last couple of weekends of this season.

'Consequently, you would have to be pretty stupid to start shouting from the rooftops about what you were going to do next season. But, we are in better shape coming back into the Premiership under Dean Richards, the director of rugby, and his coaching team.'

Quins have been recruiting hard since Christmas, and the arrival of Test centres Stuart Abbott and Hal Luscombe along with the Castres pair of Paul Volley and Nicolas Spanghero gives the first-team squad heavier hitting power. They also boast the talents of ex-Springbok captain Andre Vos and, at No. 10, former New Zealand star Andrew Mehrtens.

In recent years, Evans has swapped his desk for the training ground to help the club avoid the drop, but his luck ran out last season. 'Dean is in charge of all playing matters and my tracksuit has remained in the drawer all year!' added Evans, who now works closely with the Harlequins rugby league operation that also uses the Twickenham Stoop.

'No one had been through what we experienced last season and we had a contingency plan in place but a lot of the numbers were guestimates. It was hard to let go some really good people who weren't responsible at all for what happened and we will increase the staff numbers in a slightly different way now that were are back in the Premiership.

'It's a bigger operation in the Premiership and one of the things that helped when we

RIGHT Harlequins' former All Black fly half Andrew Mehrtens cheers on his side during their first division match away at Pertemps Bees.

FACING PAGE Dean Richards, director of rugby at Harlequins, is in charge of all playing matters.

PAGE 91 Quins celebrate promotion to the Premiership as champions of National League Division One.

went down was the new Lexus Stand which was halfway through the build. It gave everyone a boost at the start of this season because staff had new offices, the players got new dressing rooms and other important facilities, a new members bar and club shop.

'A vital point was the third game of the season – our first at home – against Newbury when we unveiled the statue of Nick Duncombe [their England scrum half who died tragically young] and opened the stand and it felt like we were still an ambitious player in English rugby. In our last season in the Premiership we capped our season tickets sales at 4,600 and 200 sponsors and that went up to 4,800 and 400 in the first division but, obviously, we cut the prices accordingly.'

Prices are now back to the level that existed before relegation blighted the club. It's been a tough road back, but Evans is convinced Quins can follow the lead of Worcester and Bristol, who forced their way into the Premiership and consolidated with some style. Of course, one club is going to be relegated at the end of next season and face the kind of problems that have torn the Leeds squad apart and seen director of rugby Phil Davies quit. It's a salutary warning to the Premiership, but Quins have proved you can bounce back and captain Vos felt a debt of honour to the club to ensure they regained top-flight status. He could have walked away having achieved his goal but will be in action in the Premiership again next season, going where only the very toughest flankers are prepared to put their bodies on the line.

Vos said: 'There is huge satisfaction at having gained promotion but the job isn't finished yet even though that may appear to be the case.

'By agreeing to stay for another year means I will have been at Quins for five years and I am still enjoying my rugby and want the chance to play in the Premiership again. Having played all my rugby in South Africa, prior to coming over in 2002, I had never had to deal with relegation and promotion. The Premiership is the toughest club/provincial tournament in the world and any team can knock over the No. 1 ranked side.

'I feel like I have got a new lease of life in terms of my rugby career and I have thoroughly enjoyed this season which has seen us receive unbelievable support from our fans and sponsors. Our feelings at gaining promotion were in total contrast to a year ago when we were relegated.

'I wouldn't wish that on anyone.'

Vos was joined in the first-team squad last season by England World Cup winner Will Greenwood and former England No. 8 Tony Diprose, who also felt honour-bound to ensure the club got back into the Premiership before retiring. As they have vacated the Quins squad, new names are being put on the back of the famous jerseys for the men who must fight off the threat of relegation this time around. They include Danny Care, who is one of the brightest scrum-half prospects in England and moved from newly relegated Leeds; Will Skinner, who left Leicester to join Quins as an aggressive back-row forward; and Chris Hala'Ufia, the 11-times-capped Tongan back-row forward, who joined Quins from Earth Titans having previously played for Parma in Italy.

With Vos adding huge experience to a squad that director of rugby Richards believes is equipped to make an impact in the Premiership, you can understand why those fans who stuck by the team have been so quick to buy their season tickets for the coming campaign. Richards is not one to boast about anything to do with rugby, but he is genuinely excited about the new international centre combination that will wear the multi-colours next season.

Richards said: 'I believe that Stuart Abbott and Hal Luscombe can be the best centre pairing in the Premiership.'

It's a very big claim, but then Richards is a very big man with a proven track record in the Premiership while in charge of Leicester. Now, he is going to try and create something special at the Twickenham Stoop.

And with men like Luscombe, Abbott, Vos and Mehrtens in the Quins armoury, the Twickenham Stoop will be a difficult place for every Premiership team to visit in the new season.

Wasps Zap Scarlets
the 2006 Powergen Cup Final
by ALASTAIR HIGNELL

'Wasps deserved their victory and, despite the rain, Dallaglio and Co. celebrated with every bit as much gusto as on previous cup-winning occasions.'

New faces, same old story. The Powergen Cup final may have featured a Welsh team for the first time, but Llanelli Scarlets were powerless to prevent London Wasps from picking up a fifth Twickenham title in four years. Lawrence Dallaglio and his men had enjoyed the run of the old stadium in lifting a Heineken Cup and three successive Premiership titles. There was something inevitable about their coronation as the last ever Powergen Cup holders.

The sponsors might have decided to focus elsewhere, but Wasps once again mirrored their captain's single-minded intensity with a display of champion quality. Llanelli started the match as underdogs and ended it well beaten. The Scarlets lacked nothing in the way of motivation. A home victory apiece in the group stages of the Heineken Cup had set this up as a decider between clubs who could lay claim to being the most successful teams in the professional era from their respective sides of the Severn. And with Llanelli supremo Gareth Jenkins set to be installed as the new Wales coach, the desire to provide the perfect send-off to a lifelong servant was intense. For a man whose playing and coaching credentials had been forged in the ancient Anglo-Welsh rivalry that, before the

arrival of national leagues, had once been the lifeblood of the club game in both countries, it would have been perfectly fitting.

Llanelli had done the hard part. They had been woefully underprepared before going into their Millennium Stadium semi-final with Bath, yet had shown great character and a proud cup fighting tradition to come from behind to snatch victory. They had continued to win key matches despite the prolonged absence of their best player, Dwayne Peel, and were quietly confident that with the backing of rugby fans across the Principality they could surprise the English champions at a stadium that had become Wasps' second home.

But Wasps had their own farewells to make. World Cup winning scrum half Matt Dawson had announced his intention to retire from rugby at the end of the season. Centre Stuart Abbott was on his way to Harlequins. And Dallaglio and the rest of England's Six Nations underachievers had points to prove to the Twickenham faithful. One of these, Tom Voyce, scored a trademark opportunist try in each half to win the game for his side. Two more England internationals – full back Mark van Gisbergen, whose two conversions and three penalties earned him a

PREVIOUS PAGE Tom Voyce crosses for one of his two tries in Wasps' 26-10 win in the final.

BELOW Simon Shaw plucks the ball out of the Twickenham air for Wasps.

personal haul of 13 points, and Alex King, with a late dropped goal – completed Wasps' scoring. For Llanelli, full back Barry Davies scored an early try while outside half Mike Hercus landed one penalty and a conversion.

Heavy rain and a glut of individual errors reduced the

game as a spectacle while Wasps' iron-fisted forward dominance ensured that, the early Scarlets' salvo aside, the occasion never really hit the heights as a showpiece. The rhythm of the match was also interrupted by injuries. Ireland's Triple Crown winning flankers Jonny O'Connor of Wasps and Scarlets' skipper Simon Easterby both suffered severe neck injuries, while referee Alan Lewis failed to reappear after the interval, having hurt his leg during a 57-minute first half.

O'Connor was carried off after less than a minute's play. A misjudged head-on tackle on Llanelli's rampaging No. 8 Alix Popham necessitated five minutes' treatment on the pitch before O'Connor was sent to hospital in a neck brace and on a stretcher. Worst fears were mercifully unrealised both for O'Connor and Easterby, whose team-mate Mark Jones provided emergency treatment during play before the arrival of the medical team for another seven anxious minutes' wait.

In between the injuries, Llanelli opened up a lead when a sniping break from scrum half Clive Stuart-Smith – starting in place of injured Lions star Dwayne Peel – found support from Inoke Afeaki and Gavin Thomas before Barry Davies' stunning finish under the posts gave Hercus the simplest of conversions. Hercus and van Gisbergen then exchanged penalties as the errors multiplied and Wasps prop Ali McKenzie completed a

mad ten minutes by squandering a three-man overlap before earning a yellow card for failing to release the ball at a ruck. Wasps, though, were beginning to take control, although they still needed an interception – made by Jeremy Staunton, supported by the speedy Voyce – to earn the try that, with van Gisbergen's conversion, ensured half-time parity at 10-10.

Voyce's second try – after a slashing break from Abbott had left both Hercus and Davies in his wake – highlighted once again both the wing's speed and his sense of anticipation. As the heavens opened and rain lashed down on Twickenham, that score was pretty much the last event of meaning. The Scarlets, resigned to living off scraps of possession, were forced to play catch-up rugby. All Wasps had to do was turn the screw up front – and kick their goals. Two more penalties by van Gisbergen and Alex King's late dropped goal washed away all chances of an upset, bringing the final score to 26-10.

Wasps deserved their victory and, despite the rain, Dallaglio and Co. celebrated with every bit as much gusto as on previous cup-winning occasions. Although the Scarlets didn't quite measure up

on the day, their presence at Twickenham was important. The knockout tournament's reinvention as a cross-border competition had not initially been received with much enthusiasm. Bristol's decision to rest their first team for the pool stages – in order to focus all their energies on avoiding relegation from the Premiership – might have been the most blatant example, but from the starting line-ups announced by other English clubs, it was clear that they, too, had downgraded the competition. The Welsh clubs also found their resources stretched too thinly. The quality of the tournament had deservedly been called into question.

Without two superb semi-finals – Wasps beat Leicester in the other Millennium Stadium showdown – those questions would have received a far greater airing. Without Llanelli's appearance in the final, they might have become unanswerable. New competitions always take time to grab the imagination of the public. Even the Heineken Cup was slow off the blocks. The Powergen Cup – or whatever the name of the trophy that Wasps will defend next year – has been given much-needed breathing space by Llanelli Scarlets.

Strength in teamwork

Clifford Chance is pleased to support Wooden Spoon.

Our mission is grounded in the belief that we have a responsibility as a business
to contribute to our communities. For further details see our website:
www.cliffordchance.com/community

CLIFFORD
CHANCE

www.cliffordchance.com

Munster at Last
the 2006 Heineken Cup Final
by ALASTAIR HIGNELL

'Most of them, however, must have watched with a grim fascination as Biarritz initially threatened to write another chapter in that ever-expanding book of heroic failures.'

A phenomenon came to Cardiff and painted the town red. Munster's legendary army of fans took possession of the Welsh capital and, on one of the most extraordinary days in recent rugby history, roared their team to the victory they had long considered their destiny.

The Heineken Cup has been the making of Munster. Rugby has always inspired a fanatical following in the west of Ireland, but the pan-European tournament has turned a crowd into a multitude. While Thomond Park remained sold out and impregnable – Munster have never lost a European match at the stadium – away matches became modern-day pilgrimages. Since 1999, when Munster reached the quarter-finals for the first time, they have been followed in ever greater numbers and, until Cardiff 2006, with ever greater desperation.

For to back Munster was to embrace both triumph and heartache. In 2000 a sensational semi-final victory over Toulouse had been followed by a one-point defeat by Northampton in the final. A controversial refereeing decision cost them the semi-final against Stade Francais in 2001 while an

undetected bit of cheating by Leicester's Neil Back contributed to defeat in the 2002 final. The euphoria of the 'miracle' pool win over Gloucester in 2003 was matched by the agony of semi-final defeat to Wasps in 2004. The rest of the rugby world was beginning to wonder whether Munster's every European campaign was doomed to end in glorious failure.

The 2006 campaign looked to be following that script. Munster needed a big pool win over Sale to guarantee a home quarter-final. They got it. They had to beat Leinster in Dublin to get to the final. They did so, in brilliant fashion. Now they were up against a team that had thrashed them in 2005 before going on to pick up the French Championship. What's more, Biarritz appeared to be running into form at just the right time. Despite a pool loss to Saracens, the Basques had despatched Sale and Bath in knockout matches with quiet efficiency. They topped their own domestic league and, themselves desperate for a first ever European success, looked to have the game for every occasion. For every occasion, that is, except the one they encountered in Cardiff. Not even a French Championship final at the Stade de France could have prepared the Basques for the atmosphere at the Millennium Stadium.

For the Munster fans had converged on Cardiff in their thousands. An estimated 60,000 had descended on the city, by hook or by crook. When the Cork ferries were cancelled on Friday due to stormy weather, many intrepid supporters simply hired cars, drove ten hours to Belfast to make the shorter, more sheltered crossing to Liverpool and then raced down to Cardiff, determined to be there when their heroes finally delivered. Most of them, however, must have watched with a grim fascination as Biarritz initially threatened to write another chapter in that ever-expanding book of heroic failures. With the match less than three minutes old, centre Philippe Bidabe broke down the left and giant left wing Sireli Bobo tiptoed down the touch line to score the opening try of the match. That the TV replay suggested a foot in touch served only to convince the pessimists that once again the Fates were set to turn against the Irishmen.

PREVIOUS PAGE Peter Stringer gets away from Serge Betsen to score Munster's second try.

BELOW Oh no, not again! Sireli Bobo scores the opening try for Biarritz. Nevertheless Munster were to have the final say.

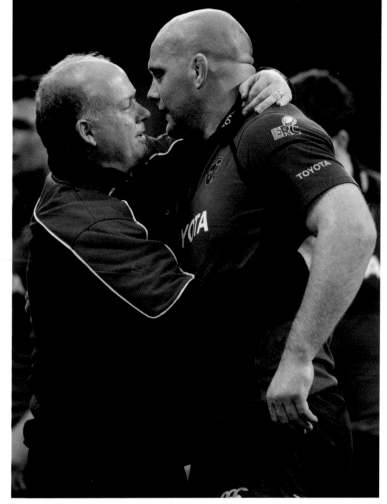

However, the majority of Munster's magnificent army are optimists. Their passionate outpourings from the stand galvanised the men in red. Ireland outside half Ronan O'Gara, a pre-match doubt with a gastric virus, popped over a penalty and then began to work the corners as Munster started to pour forward. Another clever kick into space was followed by a superb piece of skill from Anthony Horgan, while great support from Jerry Flannery and Paul O'Connell created the momentum for centre Trevor Halstead to crash over for the try that, with O'Gara's conversion, put Munster noses in front. A penalty from France scrum half Dimitri Yachvili levelled the scores again, but a moment of utter brilliance from his opposite number, Peter Stringer, turned the game on its head.

Stringer spotted that, for reasons best known to himself, Bobo had abandoned his wing at a defensive scrum. A slight wheel at the scrum gave Stringer the space to avoid Serge Betsen and race away to cross unopposed, O'Gara again converting.

Up 17-10 at half-time, Munster had the momentum as well as the belief that destiny was in sight. In a frenzied start to the second period, their aggressive defence tore into Biarritz. Big hits on Damien Traille and Serge Betsen stopped promising attacks in their tracks. Desperate chasing of kicks from O'Gara and Stringer put Thion and then Traille under extreme pressure. Superb harrying from the midfield backs pressurised centre Bidabe into throwing a pass behind wing Bobo. Paul O'Connell and Donncha O'Callaghan stole vital line-out possession on the Biarritz throw. A further penalty from O'Gara extended the lead to ten points. The French were obviously rattled. They therefore showed great skill and nerve to drag themselves back into the match. Scrum half Yachvili was again the catalyst, ably assisted by his half-back partner, Julien Peyrelongue, and the outstanding forward on either side – Imanol Harinordoquy.

Three ice-cool penalties from the scrum half had not only begun to sow the seeds of doubt in the minds of Munster's exhausted players but had also begun to quell the crowd. But a second turning point – a cutaway shot on the giant screen showing thousands of supporters in Limerick town centre – reignited the support inside the Millennium Stadium, and reinvigorated their heroes. In attack, a drive from O'Connell set up the position from which O'Gara could land his fourth penalty with seven minutes to go. In defence, a crucial intervention by Stringer averted one danger while accidental offside by Bobo ruined another promising attack. All the time, the crowd was getting noisier and noisier. When O'Gara cleared for touch deep into injury time, they were delirious. Munster were home 23-19 and the party to end all parties could begin.

Down to the Wire
the 2006 Challenge Cup Final

by TERRY COOPER

'But there was a mass of injury time and tons of Irish fighting quality. They established squatters' rights on the Gloucester line to claim the two tries they wanted to stay afloat.'

Expectations that we would be treated to a display of lovely running rugby from Gloucester and London Irish's young, gifted backs – who had been a feature of the spring – became a non-runner when rain torrented down all day. Instead, we witnessed a frenzied, passionate spectacle that left even spectators tense and breathless. The players were shattered heroes. There was an amazing recovery from Irish, a last-gasp kick that could have won the match, a winning try in extra time and more kicks at goal by Irish in a bid to steal the cup. And a true rarity – a losing coach prepared to admit that a wonderful contest could override disappointment.

BELOW Gloucester try scorer Mark Foster closes in on opposite number Topsy Ojo of London Irish.

FACING PAGE Gloucester are euphoric as the final whistle goes at the end of extra time.

The epic at Harlequins' extended Twickenham Stoop was in the tradition of memorable finals in this second-tier European event. Irish coach Brian Smith, who was forced to watch from the stand after recently criticising a referee, said: 'It might be heartbreaking for my players, but not for me. To see the spirit and skill which the team produced and to achieve mission impossible with two tries to draw level makes me proud.'

There was talk that the fixture was fairly meaningless because both clubs had qualified for the following season's Heineken Cup. The bliss on the winners' faces and the despair of the losers refuted that mischievous theory.

Irish were away with crisp efficiency through a couple of penalties from Barry Everitt in the opening ten minutes. Both sets of backs attempted genuine handling moves, but it was clear that judicious kicking was the main currency. Mike Tindall demonstrated that for the first try. He slid through a wicked diagonal and wing Mark Foster beat Topsy Ojo as they skidded for the elusive ball. Gloucester won a rare line out for their second try. Though they lost the line-out count 21-8, they made this one tell when Andy Hazell was driven over from ten yards in the 31st minute.

Instantly Irish responded when wing Delon Armitage caught Everitt's looping cross-kick. Everitt converted, Ryan Lamb replied with a penalty and Everitt opened the second half with a dropped goal. Lamb, trying something audacious, was twice heavily tackled in the upper body and departed. His coach, Dean Ryan, commented: 'They did a real job of knocking him about. He'll have ten years of that as oppositions target a match winner.'

The final quarter of normal time began with Irish down to 14 men when No. 8 Juan Manuel Leguizamon was sin-binned. The card was not expensive for Irish, who 'drew' the ten minutes 3-3, with Everitt cancelling out Ludovic Mercier's penalty. But 'Ludo' added another goal and the contest seemed neatly parcelled up for Gloucester when James Simpson-Daniel scooped up Bob Casey's pass aimed at nobody in particular and motored from his own half to score between the posts. Mercier converted, Gloucester led 31-19 and 78 minutes of real time had elapsed.

But there was a mass of injury time and tons of Irish fighting quality. They established squatters' rights on the Gloucester line to claim the two tries they wanted to stay afloat. And they exploded another rugby notion – that driving mauls and rucks are tedious. Their forwards tried to drive over 20 times in one play. The spectators were delirious, urging their hulking hordes to one more supreme effort of defence or advance. Somebody had smuggled in a bass drum, and its booming

intensified the feverish atmosphere. Kieran Roche was denied a score by the TV ref as Irish finally inched over the line, but they tried again and flanker Olivier Magne was given the try. Everitt converted and Irish staged an action replay. This time there were 11 separate surges before hooker Robbie Russell was bundled over. All square at 31-31.

Everybody expected Everitt to complete Irish's comeback with a relatively simple conversion from halfway out on the right. But the tension affected one of the most reliable kickers in the game and his shot was badly hooked. In extra time he did land a penalty before a piece of magic from centre Anthony Allen 48 seconds into the second period set up Gloucester's winner. Allen disrupted the defence, James Forrester was on the blind side of a ruck and he kicked the ball over the goal line. 'I thought I had overcooked it,' he said. 'The dead-ball line crept up and I panicked, but just got there.'

There was still time for nerves to be shredded further as poor Everitt missed a penalty and a dropped-goal attempt and Leguizamon also failed with a long drop shot in search of the three points to win the cup. As the final whistle blew with the score at 36-34, Gloucester became the sixth consecutive English winners of the trophy – which have included Sale and Wasps, who immediately went on to Premiership glory. And coach Ryan predicted: 'This new group of players will be around for a long time and we will win big games like this. This performance will provide good memories when we reach future finals. Players like Foster, Allen and Lamb might be young, but they are not rookies. They are the finished article and contributed to an afternoon of cracking entertainment.'

Gloucester reached the final by winning a group containing Bayonne, Bucharest and Toulon before overcoming Brive and Worcester in the knockout stages. Irish progressed past Pau, Parma and Agen before defeating Bayonne and Newcastle.

LEFT James Forrester enjoys the moment with the Gloucester fans after he chases down his kick ahead to score the winning try.

REACH
FOR THE BEST

It's rare to find a recruitment consultancy who tackle personnel requirements with such tenacity and unfailing dedication. An unrivalled approach that has enabled Pertemps to remain unchallenged at the top of the league as the UK's leading independent recruitment consultancy.

As market leaders, we have developed our reputation not just by "filling positions" but by adding value to our client portfolio, a philosophy which is reflected in the diverse range of leading blue-chip companies that currently utilise our services.

Operating in three service divisions: commercial and professional, industrial and driving and technical and executive, our fully integrated service ensures that we are able to deliver quality personnel with the right skills, in the right place at the right time.

So, if you are seeking to win the competition for business, make sure that you retain the competition for talent by choosing Jobs@Pertemps, Britain's most successful independent recruitment consultancy.

REVIEW OF THE
SEASON 2005-06

A French Affair
the 2006 Six Nations Championship

by CHRIS JONES

'While [the coaches'] influence was felt throughout the tournament, it was the players who created the moments of genius, desperation, anxiety and unbounded joy ...'

The RBS Six Nations Championship belonged to France by the time a season of wildly fluctuating fortunes ended. Ireland had to settle for the Triple Crown but took great solace in the fact that it was delivered courtesy of victory over England at Twickenham.

A second successive fourth-place finish for England would see the sacking of coaches Dave Alred (kicking), Phil Larder (defence) and Joe Lydon (attack) with head coach Andy Robinson somehow remaining while all those around him were axed. If the fallout from another poor England season was clearly on the cards, the departure of Mike Ruddock, the man who guided Wales to Grand Slam glory in 2005, was not.

There had been rumours about disquiet in the Welsh camp during the autumn internationals but no one expected Ruddock to be forced out of his job during the 2006 Six Nations campaign. It was a sad and tawdry affair; one that saw Ruddock depart for a new position away from rugby with his own reputation intact while those who had directly – or indirectly – helped in his departure felt the wrath of a bemused and angry Welsh nation. The affair shook the Welsh Rugby Union to its core and saw captain Gareth Thomas make the mistake of going onto local television to explain the players' stance. It was poor judgment by Thomas, whose performance under intense pressure failed to dismiss the idea that the players had not been fully behind Ruddock. Thomas, later that same day, suffered a fall at home that so badly damaged an artery in his neck that he was forced to stop playing, and doubts remain about his ability to lead Wales again, or even play the sport he loves.

It was Australian Scott Johnson who took over as head coach, having been one of Ruddock's support staff, and weeks of 'will he, won't he' followed as speculation about who would be the full-time coach remained on the front pages of Welsh newspapers. Eventually, Johnson stuck to his avowed intention to return home to Australia for family reasons, clearing the way for Gareth Jenkins, the obvious candidate for many years, to finally be allowed to take control of the national team after making such a good impression with Llanelli Scarlets and as one of the Lions midweek coaches in New Zealand in 2005.

French coach Bernard Laporte and Eddie O'Sullivan, his Irish counterpart, finished their respective campaigns in good shape, while Frank Hadden proved to be an excellent replacement for the controversial Australian Matt Williams as Scotland coach. Pierre Berbizier took over from John Kirwan as Italy coach and brought a better structure to a team that continued to come close to triumph only to fall agonisingly short.

But the RBS Six Nations campaign in 2006 was not merely about the fortunes of the various coaches. While their influence was felt throughout the tournament, it was the players who created the moments of genius, desperation, anxiety and unbounded joy that once again captivated the rugby public's attention.

There was also the running English sore created by Robinson's decision to recall former captain Lawrence Dallaglio despite the unsettling effect it was bound to have on current skipper Martin Corry. It proved to be a dilemma Robinson never came to terms with and provided an unwelcome distraction in a championship season of too many management shortcomings. By the final match against Ireland, Dallaglio was a forlorn figure, left as an unused replacement and totally frustrated on the Twickenham touch line.

France started their campaign with a completely unexpected 20-16 defeat at Murrayfield, where Hadden tapped into the pride of wearing the Scottish jersey – something Matt Williams had failed to achieve – and the response from his players was dramatic. Hadden knew where his squad was lacking and concentrated, instead, on areas where they could be truly competitive.

Italy competed well in Ireland before going down 26-16, with match commissioner Rob Flockhart investigating an alleged biting incident. Irish coach Eddie O'Sullivan claimed flanker Simon Easterby had been bitten on the arm by an Italian player in the second half. O'Sullivan said: 'A substantial mark has been left but the doctor took a look at it and said Simon is okay. We mentioned our concern to the referee but he couldn't do anything because he didn't see the incident. This shouldn't happen – there is no place in the game for things like this.' No one was found guilty.

At Twickenham, the Six Nations started with a 47-13 destruction of champions Wales, and England backed this up with a 31-16 win in

FACING PAGE Mirco Bergamasco escapes the despairing dive of Brian O'Driscoll to score for Italy against Ireland on the opening day of the 2006 Six Nations.

Rome to suggest that they could be in the mix for the title. However, the next match was at Murrayfield, where the French had been ambushed, and England's season was about to be turned on its head.

Post-Murrayfield, the French recalled veterans Raphael Ibanez and Olivier Magne for the arrival of Ireland at the Stade de France, and what unfolded was the most bizarre match of the tournament. France coach Bernard Laporte referred to the fans at the stadium as '*ces bourgeois de merde*' after his side was jeered off the field having held on to beat Ireland 43-31. Who needs enemies with friends like that?

Laporte's side were forced to repel waves of attacks, but held out for their first win of the championship. The Irish trailed 43-3 in the 59th minute but rallied to what seemed a hopeless cause so well that four unanswered tries from Ronan O'Gara, Gordon D'Arcy, Donncha O'Callaghan and Andrew Trimble dumbfounded the locals and almost caused a remarkable upset.

England arrived at Murrayfield forewarned but not forearmed. They should have taken more notice of the Scots victory against France and prepared for a mighty defensive action by the home side. It was duly delivered, led by the brilliant flanker Ally Hogg, who snuffed out numerous England attacks, and Scotland were brave 18-12 victors. Jason White, their captain, would have a marvellous season with Scotland and English champions Sale, putting his body on the line in every match. This was a Scottish triumph to stir the blood and justified the over-the-top pre-match programme featuring

extras from *Braveheart* and much waving of flaming torches. By the end of the match, England had been sent home 'tae think again'. Dallaglio, Tom Voyce and Simon Shaw were so underused against the Scots, they were able to help Wasps defeat Sale in the Guinness Premiership the next day!

With France taking nearly 60 minutes to find their game before defeating Italy 37-12, the trip to Paris offered England some hope they could erase the memory of Murrayfield. France, with Thomas Castaignede enjoying a break from the relegation worries at Saracens, were veering from the dreadful to the sublime and the arrival of Corry's men only helped focus wandering attention.

Scotland proved that if you tackled with commitment and spirit for 80 minutes you could totally nullify the England attacking game plan. The challenge for England was to prove they could turn pressure into points rather than embarrassing errors. England players claimed a fish meal had left them lethargic on match day in Paris, but that excuse didn't satisfy the thousands who had made the effort to cheer on their men at Stade de France.

The fans and England management had to witness a dreadful 31-6 loss to France, with the back division failing to create a single line break. It forced head coach Robinson to belatedly turn to Stuart Abbott, a player who looks for space to run into rather than an opponent's body, for the final match with Ireland. Abbott was one of seven new faces drafted into the England team, while, in contrast, Ireland arrived at Twickenham with an unchanged side and aiming for championship and Triple Crown success. They had beaten Wales 31-5 at Lansdowne Road and struggled to account for Scotland 15-9 in the last match at the old stadium, which is now being rebuilt, but they duly disposed of England 28-24.

Italy grabbed an 18-18 draw with Wales in Cardiff when they should have won, and then lost 10-13 at home to the battling Scots. It was a poor return for Berbizier, but the team is getting better under his control. The same could not be said for Wales, who lost their last game as reigning champions at home to France 21-16. Yet the French then had to wait until the Ireland match against England was over – it kicked off later – to receive the trophy, which meant captain Fabien Pelous was in a dinner jacket when the rest of the squad sprayed him with champagne. It was a messy end to another absorbing championship.

LEFT Centre Florian Fritz scores late in the second half against Wales in Cardiff to help secure the championship for France.

The Club Scene
England: Sale's Year

by BILL MITCHELL

'That result must have brought a sigh of relief to all those who consider a season's champions to be the club which finishes top of the table ...'

There have been happier campaigns in England – the national team fell below the high achievements of recent years and the domestic scene has been beset by political problems which are normally seen mainly in the round-ball game – that is, club versus country disputes – and at the moment there are no signs that there will be any amicable solutions.

Release of players for November international matches has been a sore point for clubs in the professional era, since the players receive their remuneration for their day jobs from the clubs, who are expected to fulfil full fixture lists in the month in question without men who are required by their countries. There has been a tacit agreement that availability would be confined to three games, but a special match against New Zealand in early November has been added to the schedule, and this has not gone down a bundle with the players' employers, who lost a court action but with an appeal still a possibility. This is not exactly a period of goodwill to exhibit to the general supporting public, who already pay high prices for matches at Twickenham and might just vote with their feet if the disputes are not settled and the top side's results do not improve, since nothing less than a Grand Slam, or at the worst the Six Nations title (or even the Triple Crown), will suffice.

Leading on from that, the season, which at one time looked full of promise for the national team, ended in near disaster, with fourth place in the Six Nations being followed by an ill-advised tour to Australia and two heavy defeats, which completed a sequence of five such horrors. It is interesting to mention that former England hooker Brian Moore in *The Daily Telegraph* picked a 2006 Six Nations team which consisted of four Scots, three Frenchmen, three Irishmen, three Italians and two Welsh players, but no one from England. This tells a sad story and one that cannot be disputed.

But it had all started well with a most promising month in November, involving good victories over Australia (26-16) and Samoa (40-3) and a possibly unlucky 23-19 loss against the New Zealand All Blacks. Even the Six Nations campaign started very well with a 47-13 victory against an admittedly depleted Welsh outfit, which was followed by a sound but less convincing performance in Rome against Italy (31-16).

Surely Scotland – even at Fortress Murrayfield – would present no serious problems, especially as their best lock, Scott Murray, was missing thanks to a short suspension. The latter punishment perhaps showed some kind of derision felt by the disciplinary committee for the arbiter's action – a thoroughly harsh red card in Cardiff when New Zealand referee Steve Walsh decided that a shocking late tackle on Murray by Wales's Ian Gough was a less serious offence than an accidental boot in the offender's face in an attempt to free trapped legs. But at least Murray did not suffer the same fate as an English official in the not too distant past, who was drenched by the contents of a cold bucket full of water dumped on him by the same Mr Walsh! Justice seen to be done?

But what ensued in the Calcutta Cup match was an evening of astonishing defending by the men in dark blue, who made 113 tackles, all of which meant that England had only one real try-scoring opportunity in the whole match, and the unfortunate Ben Cohen spilled it just before half-time with the line at his mercy. The only two near misses in terms of tries in the second half fell to the Scots, who finished worthy winners 18-12 thanks also to accurate kicking by Chris Paterson and Dan Parks.

Few changes were made for the trip to Paris, where a dreadful defensive error in the first minute set France in motion to deliver a rout (31-6). There was an improved

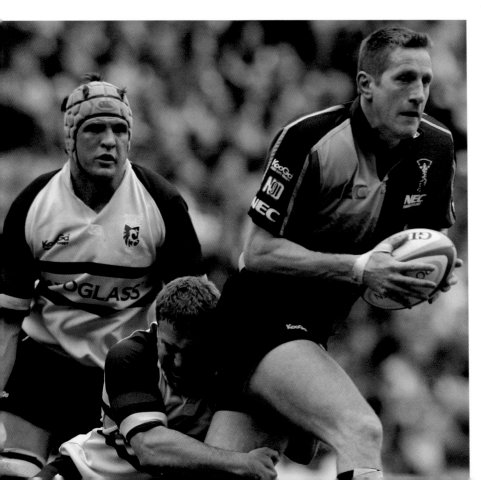

LEFT Will Greenwood in action at Twickenham one more time as Harlequins beat Bedford 39-23 to win the Powergen National Trophy.

FACING PAGE Stockport, winners of the Powergen Intermediate Cup, celebrate during finals day at Twickenham.

PREVIOUS PAGE Oriol Ripol of Sale eludes Alesana Tuilagi of Leicester to score his side's third try of the Guinness Championship final.

performance at Twickenham in the 28-24 defeat to Ireland, who even so were still the better team and missed numerous chances to score (although their first try should not have been allowed).

It was then that a most unwise trip to Australia took place with a weakened team, possibly to give players some experience at the top level. But two defeats (34-3 and 43-18) were hardly likely to give confidence boosts to callow performers, all of which brought demands for changes in the coaching staff, with the result that at the moment only the top man, coach Andy Robinson, remains in position – but for how long?

There could, however, be light at the end of a dark tunnel as England's Under 21 side did the Six Nations Grand Slam and came a creditable fifth in the Under 21 World Championship held in and won by France, while the 18 Group wrested the Four Nations title from the almost perennial winners, Wales.

Domestic honours went to Sale, who not only took the Guinness Premiership honours but also won a one-sided play-off final at Twickenham against Leicester (45-20). That result must have brought a sigh of relief to all those who consider a season's champions to be the club which finishes top of the table, with any play-offs being a money-spinning irrelevance for which, if anything, there should be another trophy.

Other Twickenham finals saw Wasps win the Powergen Cup in its Anglo-Welsh form, beating Llanelli Scarlets (26-10); Harlequins took the Powergen National Trophy against brave Bedford (39-23); Stockport lifted the Intermediate Cup by defeating Morley (11-6); and Dorking thrashed Cleobury Mortimer (46-3) to grab the Junior Vase. In the Varsity Match a good Cambridge pack was far too good for the Dark Blues, who went down 31-16, and Loughborough's men and UWIC's women were too good in the BUSA finals.

The Army remained services top dogs, with the RAF for once enjoying a victory (against the Royal Navy); Lancashire took County Championship honours in a thrilling final at Headquarters against Devon; and the best ladies sides were Saracens, the champions, and Richmond, who were the top knockout team and also the best sevens outfit. But where are the Barbarians going? Their two end-of-season matches were disastrous affairs against England (46-19) and Scotland (66-19), although they did win their five other matches versus less powerful sides. This could spell the end (for the moment, at least) of both international fixtures, but surely in these almost cynical professional times there is still a place for such a worthwhile traditional club.

REGISTERED CHARITY No. 1079316

Sport for Health

ENHANCING THE LIVES OF CHILDREN & YOUNG PEOPLE THROUGH SPORT

To fnd out more about the work of the **Saracens Foundation** and how you can support visit **www.saracens.com** or call us on **01923 204 601**

The word 'cynical' might also accompany some closing comments, since many may feel some unease about the way certain disciplinary committees – people of absolute integrity – have gone about their sentencing procedures for acts of field misconduct. But consider the evidence.

Four years ago Martin Johnson, a great captain by any standards, fell from grace in a club match and duly received a three-week suspension, which by various delaying tactics was not actually applied until after he had led England into vital but losing action in Paris; however, his sanction, when eventually operated, caused him to miss a less intense (on paper) game in Rome.

More recently Lewis Moody became the first England player to be sent off at Twickenham, and his seven-week ban meant that he was free (just in time!) to appear in his country's first Six Nations game of 2006. Meanwhile, Danny Grewcock, whose best friends would not claim a perfect disciplinary record on his behalf, has not exactly been unfortunate. A rumoured possible citing in 2005 was not pursued, leaving him free to appear against Wales in Cardiff, where he duly received a yellow card, which many thought was a lenient refereeing sanction. Then in 2006 Grewcock received a committee's warning as a result of another citing for alleged foul play. He was clear to take part in the subsequent Paris debacle, while another England squad member (Chuter), who was probably not needed for the Stade de France match, received an eight-week ban for an apparently similar offence.

This is probably all very coincidental, but it does give the possibly wrong impression that at times the needs of the England selectors take precedence over the good name of rugby football. Perhaps in future, officials (who undoubtedly have the best of honest intentions) should take this into consideration and rest a player – however much he is needed nationally – for a short period, which would give a clear message that justice is respected and being seen to be done.

And lastly, by way of a postscript, would it not be a good idea for the option of awarding a penalty try to be made available to referees if in their opinion an infringement had been committed with the direct intention of preventing a score, with 'probability' not being the only deciding factor?

> *BELOW* Scrum half Rhys Evans congratulates Nick Alberts after his try for a victorious Cambridge in the 2005-06 Varsity Match at HQ.

Scotland: Continuing Struggle

by ALAN LORIMER

'Below the layer of Edinburgh, Glasgow and the Borders, the amateur clubs remain important ... not least because the elite end supplies the proving ground for would-be professionals.'

Lack of money, lack of success and lack of an assured future. It was an all too depressingly familiar summary of Scotland's three professional clubs as rugby north of the border struggled to keep pace with more successful developments elsewhere.

Even before the season had come to a close, the clubs' bosses at Murrayfield had issued a stark warning that despite earlier assurances to the contrary, future funding could not be guaranteed. The Scottish Rugby Union, with cost-conscious chief executive Gordon McKie having taken over from predecessor Phil Anderton, made it clear that the union's priority was to reduce the current debt of £26 million. The professional clubs were thus instantly placed in the direct line of parsimony fire.

The SRU's desire is to rid themselves of the financial burden that central control of professional club rugby entails. They want an England type of club rugby to exist in Scotland where essentially, in return for flogging off their interests, they cede control of players to parties with bigger cash clout. All very well at board level, but when players are told of uncertain futures just hours before an important match then there are bound to be dire consequences. That was the situation with Border Reivers, who played their Celtic League match against Ulster at Netherdale under the mushroom cloud of an earlier meeting with Murrayfield officials. The inevitable defeat and the manner of defeat said it all.

But Borders, the poorest of the three Scottish clubs in terms of funding, reacted positively to finish their season strongly – a 43-5 win over the Dragons highlighting their fighting spirit – and so avoid, by two

LEFT Lock Opeta Palepoi takes a clean catch at the front of the line for Borders against Edinburgh. The Reivers won this Celtic League contest 23-11.

FACING PAGE Andrew Henderson charges for the line as Glasgow Warriors go down fighting 26-31 at Bath in the Heineken Cup.

places, the bottom spot in the Celtic League that had been their seemingly permanent ranking. Borders' other notable league wins were over the Ospreys, Edinburgh, Glasgow and Cardiff while in the European Challenge Cup they twice beat L'Aquila and chalked up a good home win over Brive.

Crucially in terms of Heineken Cup competition Borders ousted their domestic rivals Glasgow, whose miserable season, not helped by an enforced decampment from Hughenden to soccer ground Firhill, ended with an ignominious last-position finish in the league. It may sound like the ultimate coaching cliche, but professional rugby in Scotland is more about preparing players for national level. In which respect Borders, under the inspired guidance of former England scrum half Steve Bates, further developed hooker Ross Ford, lock Scott MacLeod and full back Calum MacRae, as well as restoring international confidence to wing Nikki Walker and full back Stuart Moffat.

For Glasgow there was little cheer. A poor Heineken campaign, bar their fighting display against Bath at the Rec, merely mirrored performances in the Celtic League. All this despite a strong start to the tri-nations club competition that included wins over Munster and Llanelli before a disappointing set of results after the turn of the year – the nadir of which was a 33-7 drubbing by Connacht in the final round – condemned Glasgow to Celtic League oblivion.

Still there were a number of positives for Glasgow, notably the return to international rugby of flanker Donnie Macfadyen, a strong hint that outside half Colin Gregor could make it to senior international standard, an elevation to the senior Scotland squad of their scrum half Sam Pinder for the two-Test tour to South Africa, excellent performances from youngsters John Beattie and John Barclay and a strong showing by the admittedly injury-prone prop Euan Murray.

Cynics will note that Edinburgh's top-of-the-Scottish-heap position correlated with their favoured funding, noticeably more generous than for the other two professional clubs. But even with their extra cash Edinburgh still failed to make any impression in Europe. They did, however, at one stage threaten to win the Celtic League, with a good set of early-season performances, notably their victories over the Ospreys, Connacht, Glasgow, the Dragons, Llanelli and Cardiff. Sadly for Edinburgh they bid farewell to their inspirational coach, Todd Blackadder, the former All Blacks captain. The likeable Kiwi, after five years with Edinburgh, first as a player and then as a coach, has returned to his native land to take up a coaching post with Marlborough/Nelson Bay.

Edinburgh may not have tasted outright success, but their high level of representation in the national side speaks for itself. But aside from their established international players, Edinburgh have developed a further crop, among them outside half Phil Godman, who has the kind of attributes needed to spark life into the stodgy back play of the Scotland side.

Below the layer of Edinburgh, Glasgow and the Borders, the amateur clubs remain important in Scottish rugby, not least because the elite end supplies the proving ground for would-be professionals. While standards at the top end remain encouragingly high, there is a worrying drop in numbers playing amateur rugby, a trend which, even more alarmingly, reaches into age-grade and schools rugby.

What provided an extra tang to the top division of the BT Premiership in the 2005-06 season was the decision to reduce its size from twelve to ten for this campaign. That meant three clubs had to be relegated from division one with just one being promoted from division two.

In the event it provided an exciting finish to a league which is overly protracted and is an inevitable victim of adverse winter conditions after the turn of the year. The luckless trio were bottom-placed Stirling County, Stewart's Melville FP and Biggar, while the promoted division two club was Dundee High School FP, whose inclusion in the top layer of the amateur game gives division one a wide geographical spread.

At the other end Glasgow Hawks successfully defended their division one title after setting a ferociously hot early pace and in the process demonstrated that being the only division one club in a large city can have its advantages. By contrast Edinburgh's talent is spread over five clubs – Heriot's, Watsonians, Boroughmuir, Stewart's Melville FP and Currie. From this quintet Watsonians, with a generous budget backing their campaign (resulting in an influx of South Africans), came closest to challenging Hawks in the BT Premiership before ultimately settling for second place. Watsonians, however, were not to be denied success in the BT Cup final at Murrayfield, the Myresiders securing a comfortable 31-15 win over Currie to finish their season on a high.

BELOW Watsonians celebrate victory over Currie in the final of the BT Cup at Murrayfield.

Wales: Season Without Leadership

by DAVID STEWART

'[Cardiff Blues'] year was headlined by the cameo appearances of the great Jonah Lomu. His home debut saw a full house on the last Saturday before Christmas.'

This was a season without leadership in the Principality, and it was reflected in the disappointing performances of its regional teams. None reached the knockout phase of the Heineken Cup. The Ospreys failed to consolidate their Celtic League-winning performance of a year earlier; the Scarlets showed predictable signs of rust and a need to rebuild; the Dragons had a fairly shocking time of it, missing out on Heineken Cup qualification so that this season for the first time Wales will have less than four sides in the competition; and the Blues, bless 'em, surprised everyone – not least their own increasingly cynical support – by finishing as the top domestic outfit in the league, albeit that fourth place was nothing to crow about.

A year earlier Wales had won a Grand Slam, and the Ospreys were impressive Celtic League champions looking poised to move into the new Liberty Stadium and on to greater things. This time around, at national level chief executive David Moffat left abruptly for 'personal reasons', Mike Ruddock was deposed as coach in a workers' revolution and the halo of Welsh captain Gareth Thomas slipped somewhat in the fallout.

At this stage, the law of unintended consequences kicked in. Gareth Jenkins, the outstanding local coach of his generation, whom the union had seemingly bent over backwards to avoid appointing previously, could no longer be ignored lest the rugby public should march in protest on the WRU offices. He took his protégé and loyal lieutenant Nigel Davies with him to look after the Welsh back line, and thus a vacancy opened up at Stradey Park. Cue the summer arrival of the prodigal son Phil Davies, returning to his own spiritual home – he captained Llanelli for five seasons – from relegated Leeds. An apparently unhappy Scott Quinnell promptly resigned as coach of the Llanelli club side, leaving fans to assume he considered himself the heir apparent.

Jenkins spoke to David Young about the prospect of taking charge of the Welsh forwards. Presumably emboldened by his outfit's progress, the former national prop and captain elected to stay put. Given the shambles the Blues have been in recent years, their late-season run – making them the seeded qualifier for the Heineken – surprised many.

Their year was headlined by the cameo appearances of the great Jonah Lomu. His home debut saw a full house on the last Saturday before Christmas. It may well have been a last hurrah, but it made an immediate impact on the gate, with youngsters flocking – with their mums and dads – to watch probably the best-known player the game has seen. The likes of Richard Webster and Rob Howley on the coaching staff (to whom insiders give much of the credit for the Blues' revival) were warm in their appreciation of the efforts the iconic player made to recover fitness after his kidney transplant.

His replacement as the Blues' cutting edge behind the scrum is Ben Blair, a former All Black full back known for his pace and the ability to play well in more than one position. That is a phrase previously used to describe skipper Rhys Williams, but sadly the local boy and fans' favourite suffered such a loss of form and confidence last term that he was dropped from the Welsh squad. The ongoing loss of Tom Shanklin, whose chronic knee injury seems career-threatening, is a rough blow. Another Kiwi, No. 8 Xavier Rush, was a key figure in the revival. Others who shone were scrum half Mike Phillips and back-rower Andrew Powell, both in the first year of transfers from the Scarlets.

Internal movement of players is regrettably uncontrolled and undirected; an internal market has been allowed to develop. Mr Moffat was lauded for reducing the union's appalling levels of debt, but he seemed oddly reluctant to grasp the nettle of central contracting, much less any form of central marketing and promotion of the regional units. While Scotland's district teams continue to have resourcing and low crowd problems, Ireland's long-established provincial system is paying dividends, with decent numbers at the turnstiles, Munster bringing home the Heineken Cup and Ulster winning the Celtic League closely pursued by Leinster and Munster.

Ulster's triumph came courtesy of a last-minute dropped goal from their stalwart David Humphreys for a 17-19 win against the Ospreys in their final game of the season. The crowd on a lovely Friday evening in late May at the Liberty Stadium was about half that which showed up for the season's opener, the so-called Clash of the Champions with Wasps. Lyn Jones's men let victory slip 10-18 on that occasion, and thus a pattern was set, along with a failure to make their new home a 'fortress'. The Ospreys allowed Leicester back into the infamous Heineken contest in December when Gavin Henson elbowed Alejandro Moreno and promising lock Ian Evans kicked backwards injuring Harry Ellis, allowing a winning lead to turn into a 15-17 defeat. Rumours of dressing-room discontent with management emerged soon afterwards.

Poor form and injury were major problems for Jones and his coaching team. Shane Williams did not hit the heights of a year before and Henson, Brent Cockbain and Ryan Jones all missed large chunks of the season. Others stepped up, with Duncan Jones being rewarded first with the leadership of Wales in Argentina and latterly of the Ospreys. Lyn Jones is a big admirer of his namesake: 'He leads by example on and off the field, knows how to read a game, has sound judgment, and has respect through the squad'. Watch out for a new talent in fly half James Hook, plus an experienced Kiwi influence via Justin Marshall and (subject to contractual issues) Jono Gibbes.

The Ospreys have assembled quite an array of talent behind the scrum with Tal Selley and Lee Byrne switching from the Scarlets. Quite where the funding for all this comes from is the subject of speculation in the Swansea-Neath area – the iconic Marshall was signed for a hefty fee in the face of competition once Leeds were relegated. That James Bater, a hard, old-fashioned 'dog' of a wing forward raised locally, went the opposite way, to Stradey, caused some angst – was he sacrificed to make way for Maori captain Gibbes?

Why is the Welsh national coach not granted a say about where those he may wish to select play their rugby? An example is that the Ospreys have three international hookers – Barry Williams, Huw Bennett and Richard Hibbard – on their books while the Blues and Dragons struggle for depth in that position. Gareth Jenkins, not always an uncritical co-operator with his predecessors, at least has recognised the need for a better dialogue with the regional coaches: 'We want the right relationships, and need a comprehensive programme'. The ongoing failure to centrally contract will limit his scope for achievement in that regard.

*PAGE **127*** Look familiar? Jonah Lomu hands off Emiliano Mulieri as Cardiff Blues inflict a 25-10 Heineken Cup defeat on Calvisano on Italian turf.

BELOW Dragons captain Jason Forster (now a coach at Doncaster) scores in his side's 32-18 win over Glasgow Warriors in the Celtic League.

One of the more enlightened is the Dragons' supremo, Paul Turner. A highly talented fly half at the Newbridge and Newport clubs, he sees the wisdom of embracing the regional concept in its true form; in his case, reaching out to potential support north of the M4 and into the Monmouthshire valleys – that is, beyond those who have been coming to Rodney Parade for years and seem unbothered about others joining them. Turner's problem is he needs a squad of players capable of producing football that interests the casual fan. His budget from the WRU is consistent with the other regions but the handsome 'top-up' once provided by former benefactor Tony Brown is long gone, and with it now the likes of Hal Luscombe (to Harlequins).

Turner is known to have warned his regional board that his team was running on empty two weeks in advance of the crucial European play-off game against Parma. A wafer-thin squad (club players were on the bench) was insufficient as the Italians saw them off 15-24 at Rodney Parade, and so Wales will have a mere three entrants in the Heineken for the first time.

The Dragons were put in the position of playing off for a Heineken spot because of their eighth place in the Celtic League, the lowest Welsh finish. That the Scarlets came sixth (the Ospreys were seventh) out of eleven teams shows graphically that they are a unit in transition. The modest

summer signings by Phil Davies suggest the money pot at Stradey is not overflowing, but the return of the outstanding Stephen Jones from France is a huge fillip (US Eagle Mike Hercus moves across to Rodney Parade). Is there a better half-back combination at this level in the world game than Jones and Dwayne Peel?

Simon Easterby, fresh from his endeavours with the Lions, was an effective leader. It was ironic that his season ended at Twickenham when demonstrating traditional courage on the ground (and getting a kick in the head for his pains) in the inaugural Anglo-Welsh Cup final against Wasps, ultimately in a losing cause (10-26) that day. One of the Scarlets' heroes that afternoon, as he was all season, was the evergreen tight-head John Davies. How he has not played more international football in recent years is a mystery not only to the Stradey faithful.

But then, use of playing – and monetary – resources has not been a strong point of the administration of the Welsh game since the regional set-up was put in place.

LEFT The evergreen John Davies with the Man of the Match award won for his performance in the Scarlets' 21-13 Heineken Cup pool-stage win over Wasps at Stradey Park.

Ireland: Season of Success

by SEAN DIFFLEY

'Celebrations in the Leinster dressing rooms at Murrayfield were suddenly muted when the news came in that David Humphreys ... had dropped a winning goal ...'

It's been quite a season, has 2005-06, for Irish rugby – the Triple Crown celebrated at Twickenham with that clinching victory over England; the Heineken Cup success for Munster; and the Celtic League triumph of Ulster. Ulster were closely followed in the Celtic table by Leinster and Munster in a dramatic finish. There were Leinster in Scotland, racking up their four tries for a bonus only to be frustrated in the last minute by Ulster in their simultaneous clash with the Ospreys. Celebrations in the Leinster dressing rooms at Murrayfield were suddenly muted when the news came in that David Humphreys, from an extraordinary distance, had dropped a winning goal and given Ulster the title. It was a fitting gesture from Humphreys, who had earlier announced that he was retiring from international football. His contribution to Ireland in recent times has made him a most popular figure at Lansdowne Road and elsewhere, and if he is no longer to don the green jersey, he will, hopefully, remain a stalwart in the white of Ulster.

For Leinster it was a strange season, a mystifying mixture of fantastic success – vide Toulouse – and then the total obliteration at Lansdowne Road in the Heineken semi-final by the power, skill and

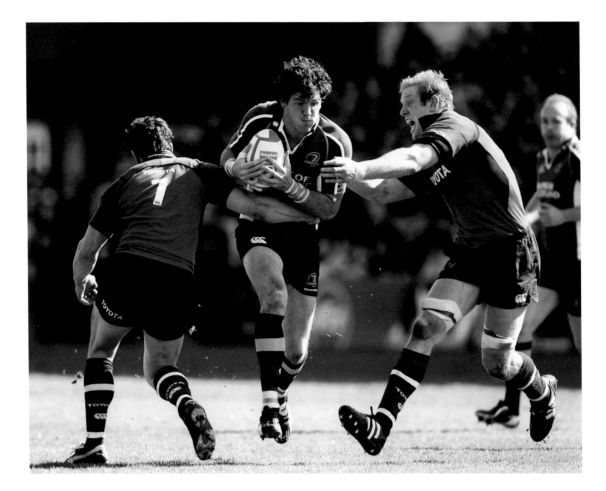

determination of Munster. The eagerly awaited all-Irish semi-final packed out the 50,000 capacity of Lansdowne. Leinster's ability to fashion tries from their talented back division, so well demonstrated in Toulouse, had many making them favourites. Munster might well have noted forward strength, but their backs, it was widely believed, wouldn't be capable of containing their Leinster counterparts. Brian O'Driscoll, Gordon D'Arcy, Shane Horgan, Felipe Contepomi and company, one of the best back divisions anywhere, would surely carve gaps in the Munster rearguard.

But it didn't turn out like that. The Munster forwards dominated and gave no opportunity to O'Driscoll and company. Donncha O'Callaghan was particularly good amidst the Munster marauders, and such Leinster luminaries as Malcolm O'Kelly were consigned, totally, to the ha'penny place. In the end the comprehensive win was 30-6, and the sea of red of Munster fans got ready for the final with Biarritz in the Millennium Stadium.

It was from those Munster fans yet another demonstration of their extraordinary support, which has gained them the accolade of the best and most well-behaved fans in the game. When so-called fans in other codes can disgrace themselves, the Munster supporters deserve every credit for their good-natured contributions to sporting harmony.

This was Munster's third Heineken European Cup final. Their record is quite remarkable. Since 1999, when they reached the quarter-finals against Colomiers, a last-eight place is the very least they have achieved. In 2000 they were beaten by Northampton in the final, in the following season they lost to Stade Francais in the semis, and in 2002 they lost to Leicester in their second final. Then followed the 2003 semi-final defeat to Toulouse, a loss the following season to Wasps at the same stage, a quarter-final defeat to Biarritz in 2005 – and then, 2006 and the third final.

The reaction to the win was quite something. The squad arrived back immediately from Cardiff, and on arrival at Shannon in the small hours they were greeted by thousands. Then followed city-wide receptions in Limerick and Cork and a grand finale of receptions at Thomond Park after their final Celtic League match of the season against Cardiff.

And how well will it all serve Munster and Irish rugby? What the Munster players chorused in all the post-match interviews was that the European Cup victory of 2006 was not 'an end. A great finish, a completion. It's only a start'. Captain Anthony Foley, Paul O'Connell and Ronan O'Gara, especially, were all anxious to make the point, and the great hope was that the reaction would encourage clubs and teams to build on the success.

While the professional game in Ireland was clearly on the crest of a wave, the situation on a lower level, among the clubs in the All Ireland League and its three divisions, was not as happy. Most are finding the financial going very tough indeed. Clubs are giving the impression that they are all amateurs but there is every indication that club coaches and some players are being paid. The presence at club level of many players from the southern hemisphere would suggest that money is changing hands. And many clubs are fielding fewer teams each weekend because of a lack of playing resources. It's a headache for the IRFU, who have yet to come up with any solution to a problem that is a strong threat to the future of the game.

In the first division of the AIB All Ireland League the top four were Garryowen, Clontarf, Cork Constitution and Shannon, and the semi-finals between them produced a final of Shannon and the Dublin side Clontarf. Well, Shannon, who have not lost an All Ireland League final since 1981 – they have been in five – once again demonstrated that they are the best side in Ireland, beating a gallant Clontarf 30-3.

An interesting titbit is the story of Jerry Flannery, the Ireland hooker and undisputed discovery of the year. He gained his chance for Munster and Ireland due to the injury to Frankie Sheahan and he certainly justified his selection. The hard-working, aggressive and skilful line-out thrower not only participated in the Irish Triple Crown success and the Munster European Cup triumph but he was also a member of All Ireland League winners Shannon. Surely a unique treble.

France: Biarritz Do It Again

by CHRIS THAU

'Could Toulouse redeem themselves by producing against the reigning champions an act of the escapism for which they have become famous … ? The answer was an emphatic no …'

The tale of the two neighbouring clubs – the 'Princes' and champions of France, Biarritz Olympique, and the bottom-of-the-league 'Paupers', Aviron Bayonnais – who finished the championship at the opposite ends of the table, is instructive. The two towns, which are geographically entwined, draw on roughly the same public support and sponsorship resources as well as the same cultural heritage.

But then Biarritz assimilated the rigours of professional rugby probably better than many French clubs, as well as enjoying the considerable advantage of being managed by Marcel Martin, arguably the most astute financial wizard in French club rugby, and being sponsored by Serge Kampf's Cap Gemini, and moved fast to capitalise on their rising status and success by adding Pays Basque (Basque Country) to their name, obviously with an eye to the commercial and public potential of the Spanish Basque country.

Bayonne, on the other hand, have struggled to retain their top-flight status at a time when Biarritz have won trophy after trophy. It is no secret that it was the Bayonne club who had been universally regarded as the heirs in French rugby of Basque rugby culture and traditions. But then nothing breeds confidence like success. And when Biarritz, champions of France, pounced on the vacant name and added it to theirs, therefore increasing their marketability and commercial potential, Bayonne had to keep a stiff upper lip and carry on with their survival plans. Mind you, it is perhaps worth noting that Bayonne have been the only club among the so-called 'minnows' in the elite section of French professional rugby to beat both Toulouse and Biarritz, which speaks volumes about their pride and obviously unfulfilled potential.

So while Biarritz demolished Toulouse 40-13, the largest scoring margin in the history of the French Championship final, to win their fifth Bouclier de Brennus amid ecstatic scenes at the Stade de France in Paris, Bayonne's players, officials and 14,000 spectators waited in silence in the town's Jean Dauger Stadium for three long minutes at the end of their 19-24 defeat by Clermond-Ferrand, listening to the radio commentary of the match between Pau and Castres, on which their fate and survival in the first division (Top 14) depended.

Another try for Pau in the closing stages of a closely fought match would have added the vital bonus points to enable them to move ahead of Bayonne and avoid relegation. In the end Romain Teulet's penalty in injury time saved Bayonne's bacon and sent Pau tumbling into the second division, while securing Castres seventh place in the table and with it a lucrative slot in the next year's Heineken Cup. Not a bad ending for the last stage of the French league as far as genuine drama is concerned. A cursory look into the crystal ball suggests that while Biarritz may well replace Toulouse as the in club of the 21st century, Bayonne will slowly descend into oblivion, according to the unforgiving law of professional rugby, 'The strong get stronger while the weak get weaker'.

The semi-final stage of the Top 14 featured two mouthwatering fixtures – Toulouse v Stade Francais and Biarritz v Perpignan, arguably the most successful quartet of French clubs during the past few years. In the event, the 30,000 spectators in Lyon and 28,000 in Montpellier, as well as many more millions glued to their TV sets, were treated to two tryless turn-offs, which, although vastly dissimilar in terms of match structure, were identical in terms of modest entertainment value, final scorelines (12-9) and score types – each team scored three penalties, with Jean-Francois Dubois for Toulouse and Julien Dupuy for Biarritz each adding a dropped goal after more than 70 minutes of playing time.

So to the final! Could Toulouse redeem themselves by producing against the reigning champions an act of the escapism for which they have become famous during the previous century of success? The answer was an emphatic no, with Pelous and his men sinking to an all-time low in a match controlled throughout by the Basques. The Biarritz front row, Petru Balan, captain Benoit August and Benoit Lecouls and his replacement Census Johnston were immovable, the locks Jerome Thion and Olivier Olibeau and his replacement David Couzinet 'did the necessary', while the back row of Imanol Harinordoquy, Thierry Dusautoir and Serge Betsen reigned supreme, allowing scrum half Dimitri Yachvili complete control of the proceedings and a hand in the five Biarritz tries.

The visible hero of the Biarritz onslaught was centre Damien Traille, who cut the Toulouse defence to shreds during a glorious spell of about 20 minutes at the beginning of the second half, making the break that led to Jean-Baptiste Gobelet's first try, scoring the second and making a contribution to Harinordoquy's try towards the end. Meanwhile, referee Didier Mene had literally a field day, being totally inconspicuous and efficient and enjoying himself as the match wore on.

Game, set and match to Biarritz, who won their fifth title, their second in consecutive years; Toulouse, meanwhile, still the reference club in French rugby, lost their seventh final.

A few days later, many of the participants in the French Championship final joined forces on the green fields of Bucharest for a warm-up Test against Romania on their way to South Africa for the end-of-season clash with the Springboks. Fabien Pelous led France to an emphatic 62-14 win over Sorin Socol's men to set the scene for the match in Cape Town a week later. Les Bleus finished the season in style with a glorious 36-26 win, with new fly half Damien Traille seemingly unstoppable. Biarritz to the fore again!

RIGHT AND BELOW Celebrations in Biarritz after the French Championship final victory over Toulouse. Serge Blanco and Marcel Martin show off the Bouclier de Brennus, while the team enjoy an open bus ride.

Italy: Searching for Talent Far and Wide

by CHRIS THAU

'The fact that his top players are actively sought by Europe's leading clubs must be good news for the Italian coach as he prepares the country for ... next year's World Cup ...'

Although Parma, with two clubs (Overmach and SKG Gran) in the semi-finals of the league, has become Italy's leading rugby stronghold, the closing stage of the championship had a predictable outcome, with eternal foes Benetton Treviso (coached by Craig Green) and Ghial Calvisano (coached by Andrea Cavinato) meeting in the final at Monza. A try by Benetton's English left wing Stuart Legg made the difference in a tense game, won by Treviso 17-12, with the rest of the points being kicked by team-mate Andrea Marcato and Calvisano's Herkie Kruger.

It was Benetton's twelfth title in the seventy-sixth championship final, and the quality of the football, as well as the fact that the two clubs dominate Italian domestic rugby overwhelmingly, must concern Italian planners and managers. They feel that once one of the Parma clubs is able to become the third genuine challenger for the title, then the national coaches will be able to operate from a position of increased strength. But until then, the national coach has to look far and wide for talent to plug the obvious gaps at top international level.

Treviso's performance was orchestrated by their new outside half, Andrea Marcato, whose contribution was noted by Italian national coach Pierre Berbizier, who selected the former Padua player for the summer tour to Japan and Fiji. Berbizier, aware of the shallow powerbase of Italian rugby, has been busily searching for talent and there

LEFT Fly half Andrea Marcato, seen here making his Italy debut as a replacement against Japan in Tokyo in June, scored 12 points in Benetton Treviso's championship final success as well as orchestrating his side's performance.

is method as well as shrewd thinking in everything the former French scrum half, captain and coach is trying to do.

During the past season, Berbizier's attention for detail has had the desired effect on the Italian team as a whole and on individuals who previously, due to a comparatively lax coaching environment, had failed to fulfil their promise. At the end of the day, Berbizier has always observed that the limitations of a team are the limitations of the players themselves. 'The better they play, the better the results will be,' he used to say, somehow paraphrasing his former mentor and coach, the prematurely departed Jacques Fouroux, whose 'Let's play well and win, in that order' had achieved a great deal of notoriety in his day.

As a result Italy's remarkable winter campaign – arguably their best since they joined the Six Nations – during which they drew with Wales in Cardiff and came close to beating both Scotland and Ireland, not to mention exposing England's limitations, has had an immediate impact on the market value of the Italian players, with several of them landing lucrative contracts with English Premiership and French Top 14 clubs. Sergio Parisse joined the Bergamasco brothers at Stade Francais, Andrea Masi has signed for Biarritz, Salvatore Perugini has joined Toulouse, Fabio Ongaro will play for the Saracens while captain Marco Bortolami has been recruited by Gloucester.

The fact that his top players are actively sought by Europe's leading clubs must be good news for the Italian coach as he prepares the country for the challenges of next year's World Cup, where a place in the quarter-finals should not be beyond their capabilities. It is good news mainly because his leading players will be exposed to elevated standards of rugby in the build-up. Yet, with the professional clubs in France and England in an increasingly militant mood, the dispute between club and country may well affect Italy's preparations for the first time, something Berbizier can well do without.

Berbizier has wasted no time in looking for reinforcements across the world. He is desperately aware that in pursuit of success the elusive edge in a match is given by a number of factors, the quality of the players available being definitely one. Given the time frame, he has been trying to avoid the predicament of his predecessor, John Kirwan, who kept changing players until a week before the World Cup tournament kicked off in 2003. In his quest for quality, Berbizier has ruffled a few feathers, including some in his native France, where his invitation to a French hopeful, former Under 21 full back David Bortolussi, to play for Italy has triggered off a fair amount of controversy.

But then controversy and adversity have followed Berbizier since the early days of his extended career as player, media pundit and coach. During his playing days, he was incessantly and unfavourably compared, by a superficial and utterly partisan press, to the flamboyant Jerome Gallion. That was as unfair as it was hurtful since he had become the influential playmaker of the French team. Berbizier's playing career came to an abrupt end when he was unceremoniously dumped following disagreements with new coach Daniel Dubroca.

Berbizier covered the 1991 World Cup as an astute pundit, and some argued that the decision to drop him for the youthful Fabien Galthie cost France a place in the final stages of the tournament and maybe a shot at the world title. He re-emerged as national coach in 1993 to take France, after winning tours to South Africa and New Zealand, to a well-deserved bronze medal in the 1995 World Cup, which France could have won. Then he was again given the push as his disagreements with the FFR became public knowledge.

So it was unlikely that controversy would prevent the single-minded perfectionist from achieving his aim. His talent scouts travelled Down Under and warned him that Penrith ARL scrum half Craig Gower had an Italian passport. Shortly afterwards, Craig's manager, Greg Willett, confirmed that an approach from a rugby union club had been made for a possible transfer of the rugby league star to Europe. Craig, who has dual Australian/Italian nationality, could well represent Italy in next year's Rugby World Cup. If he did, he would be the second Australian rugby league player to play for Italy, as former Cronulla back Nick Zisti played for the Azzurri in the 1999 tournament.

In addition to Gower and Bortolussi, Berbizier has also given the nod to both Benjamin De Jager, a wing threequarter from Amatori Catania qualified through residency, and Fabio Staibano, a prop from Parma, who won their first caps against Japan. Berbizier knows that the proof of the pudding is in the eating, so he is carefully fine-tuning his squad for the RWC 2007 qualifying matches in the autumn of 2006, a sound launching platform for the 2007 challenge.

A Summary of the Season 2005-06

by BILL MITCHELL

INTERNATIONAL RUGBY

NEW ZEALAND TO BRITISH ISLES
NOVEMBER 2005

Opponents	Results
WALES	W 41-3
IRELAND	W 45-7
ENGLAND	W 23-19
SCOTLAND	W 29-10

Played 4 Won 4

AUSTRALIA TO EUROPE
NOVEMBER 2005

Opponents	Results
FRANCE	L 16-26
ENGLAND	L 16-26
IRELAND	W 30-14
WALES	L 22-24

Played 4 Won 1 Lost 3

SOUTH AFRICA TO SOUTH AMERICA & EUROPE
NOVEMBER 2005

Opponents	Results
ARGENTINA	W 34-23
WALES	W 33-16
FRANCE	L 20-26

Played 3 Won 2 Lost 1

SAMOA TO BRITAIN
NOVEMBER 2005

Opponents	Results
SCOTLAND	L 11-18
Cambridge Univ	W 22-9
ENGLAND	L 3-40

Played 3 Won 1 Lost 2

ENGLAND TO AUSTRALIA
JUNE 2006

Opponents	Results
AUSTRALIA	L 3-34
AUSTRALIA	L 18-43

Played 2 Lost 2

IRELAND TO NEW ZEALAND & AUSTRALIA
JUNE 2006

Opponents	Results
NEW ZEALAND	L 23-34
NEW ZEALAND	L 17-27
AUSTRALIA	L 15-37

Played 3 Lost 3

SCOTLAND TO SOUTH AFRICA
JUNE 2006

Opponents	Results
SOUTH AFRICA	L 16-36
SOUTH AFRICA	L 15-29

Played 2 Lost 2

WALES TO ARGENTINA
JUNE 2006

Opponents	Results
ARGENTINA	L 25-27
ARGENTINA	L 27-45

Played 2 Lost 2

ITALY TO PACIFIC
JUNE 2006

Opponents	Results
JAPAN	W 52-6
FIJI	L 18-29

Played 2 Won 1 Lost 1

OTHER INTERNATIONAL MATCHES

Japan	44	Spain	29
Wales	11	Fiji	10
France	50	Canada	6
Scotland	19	Argentina	23
Italy	48	Tonga	0
France	43	Tonga	8
Italy	22	Argentina	39
Ireland	43	Romania	12
Italy	23	Fiji	3
Romania	14	France	62
South Africa	26	France	36
Argentina	19	New Zealand	25

ROYAL BANK OF SCOTLAND SIX NATIONS CHAMPIONSHIP 2006

Results

Ireland	26	Italy	16
England	47	Wales	13
Scotland	20	France	16
France	43	Ireland	31
Italy	16	England	31
Wales	28	Scotland	18
France	37	Italy	12
Scotland	18	England	12
Ireland	31	Wales	5
Wales	18	Italy	18
Ireland	15	Scotland	9
France	31	England	6
Italy	10	Scotland	13
Wales	16	France	21
England	24	Ireland	28

Final Table

	P	W	D	L	F	A	Pts
France	5	4	0	1	148	63	8
Ireland	5	4	0	1	131	97	8
Scotland	5	3	0	2	78	81	6
England	5	2	0	3	120	106	4
Wales	5	1	1	3	80	135	3
Italy	5	0	1	4	72	125	1

CHURCHILL CUP

Pool Stage

United States	13	Ireland A	28
England Saxons	7	Scotland A	13
Canada	10	Scotland A	15
United States	6	NZ Maori	74
Canada	11	England Saxons	41
Ireland A	6	NZ Maori	27

Bowl Final

Canada	33	United States	18

Plate Final

Ireland A	30	England Saxons	27

Cup Final

New Zealand Maori	52	Scotland A	17

PACIFIC 5 NATIONS 2006

Junior All Blacks	56	Samoa	12
Tonga	24	Fiji	23
Samoa	53	Japan	9
Junior All Blacks	38	Tonga	10
Fiji	23	Samoa	20
Junior All Blacks	38	Japan	8
Samoa	36	Tonga	0
Japan	15	Fiji	29

Champions: Junior All Blacks

'A' INTERNATIONALS

Italy	13	England	57
France	20	Ireland	12
France	44	Italy	0
France	26	England	22

OTHER RESULT

South Africa	30	World XV	27

UNDER 21 SIX NATIONS CHAMPIONSHIP 2006

Results

England	26	Wales	18
Ireland	34	Italy	9
Scotland	0	France	37
Italy	3	England	48
France	29	Ireland	10
Wales	34	Scotland	24
Scotland	22	England	49
France	51	Italy	5
Ireland	13	Wales	14
France	17	England	30
Ireland	21	Scotland	24
Wales	36	Italy	3
Wales	8	France	17
Italy	14	Scotland	21
England	40	Ireland	5

Final Table

	P	W	D	L	F	A	Pts
England	5	5	0	0	168	81	10
Wales	5	4	0	1	110	83	8
France	5	3	0	2	165	74	6
Scotland	5	2	0	3	91	155	4
Ireland	5	1	0	4	108	122	2
Italy	5	0	0	5	47	173	0

UNDER 21 WORLD CHAMPIONSHIP 2006

(Held in June in France)

Eleventh-place Play-off

Italy	12	Georgia	9

Ninth-place Play-off

Fiji	21	Scotland	19

Seventh-place Play-off

Argentina	28	Wales	12

Fifth-place Play-off

England	32	Ireland	8

Third-place Play-off

New Zealand	39	Australia	36

Final

France	24	South Africa	13

UNDER 19 WORLD CHAMPIONSHIP 2006

(Held in April in the UAE)

Eleventh-place Play-off

Japan	13	Romania	13

(Japan win after penalty shoot-out)

Ninth-place Play-off

Samoa	12	Scotland	18

Seventh-place Play-off

Argentina	26	South Africa	7

ARE PROUD TO SUPPORT

WOODEN SPOON RUGBY WORLD '07

Fifth-place Play-off

Ireland	20	Wales	15

Third-place Play-off

France	12	England	12
(England win on try count)			

Final

New Zealand	13	Australia	17

HOME NATIONS UNDER 19 COMPETITION

Champions
England

UNDER 19 INTERNATIONALS

Scotland	6	France	15
England	10	Wales	13
Wales	48	Scotland	10
Italy	26	England	34
France	20	England	17

STUDENT AND OTHER MATCHES

Scotland Students	11	England Students	73
France Amateurs	16	England Counties	29
Scotland U18	5	French Schools	25

YOUTH RESULTS

Scotland	15	France	12
Italy	15	Scotland	29
Italy	0	Scotland	15

WOMEN'S SIX NATIONS CHAMPIONSHIP 2006

Results

England	38	Wales	15
Ireland	25	Spain	3
Scotland	3	France	23
Spain	3	England	86
France	32	Ireland	0
Wales	5	Scotland	0
Ireland	7	Wales	14
Scotland	5	England	22
France	0	England	28
Wales	10	Spain	0
Ireland	0	Scotland	9
England	39	Ireland	10
Spain	12	Scotland	16
Wales	11	France	10
France	38	Spain	0

Champions: England P 5 W5; Wales P5 W4 L1;
France P5 W3 L2; Scotland P5 W2 L3; Ireland P 5
W1 L4; Spain P5 L5

IRB SEVENS SERIES FINALS 2005-06

Dubai

England	28	Fiji	26

South Africa (George)

Fiji	21	Argentina	19

New Zealand (Wellington)

Fiji	27	South Africa	22

United States (Los Angeles)

England	38	Fiji	5

Hong Kong

England	26	Fiji	24

Singapore

Fiji	40	England	19

France (Paris)

South Africa	33	Samoa	12

London (Twickenham)

Fiji	54	Samoa	14

IRB Sevens Champions: Fiji

COMMONWEALTH GAMES SEVENS 2006

(Held at Melbourne, Australia)

Final

New Zealand	29	England	21

TRI-NATIONS 2006

New Zealand	32	Australia	12
Australia	49	South Africa	0
New Zealand	35	South Africa	17
Australia	9	New Zealand	13
Australia	20	South Africa	18
New Zealand	34	Australia	27
South Africa	26	New Zealand	45
South Africa	21	New Zealand	20

New Zealand are 2006 Tri-Nations Champions

We touch down all over the USA

▶▶ **FLIGHTS FROM LONDON, MANCHESTER AND EDINBURGH**

delta.com/uk

CLUB, COUNTY AND DIVISIONAL RUGBY

ENGLAND (including Anglo-Welsh competitions)

Club Champions Challenge Match (2005)
Ospreys   12   Wasps   18

Powergen Anglo-Welsh Cup
Semi-finals
Wasps	22	Leicester	17
Llanelli	27	Bath	26

Final
Llanelli   10   Wasps   26

Guinness Premiership
	P	W	D	L	F	A	BP	Pts
Sale	22	16	1	5	573	444	8	74
Leicester	22	14	3	5	518	415	6	68
London Irish	22	14	0	8	493	454	10	66
Wasps	22	12	3	7	527	447	10	64
Gloucester	22	11	1	10	483	385	13	59
Northampton	22	10	1	11	464	488	11	53
Newcastle	22	9	1	12	416	433	9	47
Worcester	22	9	1	12	451	494	9	47
Bath	22	9	1	12	441	494	8	46
Saracens	22	8	1	13	433	483	12	46
Bristol	22	8	1	13	393	445	7	41
Leeds	22	5	0	17	363	573	8	28

Guinness Premiership Play-offs
Semi-finals
Sale	22	Wasps	12
Leicester	40	London Irish	8

Final
Leicester   20   Sale   45

National Leagues
Division One Champions: Harlequins
Runners-up: Bedford
Division Two Champions: Moseley
Runners-up: Waterloo
Division Three (N) Champions: Bradford & Bingley
Runners-up: Nuneaton
Division Three (S) Champions: Cambridge RFC
Runners-up: North Walsham

Powergen National Trophy
Quarter-finals
Exeter	23	Earth Titans	8
Harlequins	37	Plymouth Albion	24
Nottingham	34	London Welsh	3
Otley	13	Bedford	14

Semi-finals
Exeter	25	Bedford	27
Nottingham	10	Harlequins	24

Final
Bedford   23   Harlequins   39

Powergen Intermediate Cup Final
Stockport   11   Morley   6

Powergen Junior Vase Final
Dorking   46   Cleobury Mortimer   3

County Championship Final
Lancashire   32   Devon   26

County Championship Shield Final
Cheshire   32   Middesex   17

County Championship Plate Final
Notts, Lincs, Derbys   21   Oxfordshire   17

University Match
Oxford U   16   Cambridge U   31
University U21 Match
Oxford U U21   23   Cambridge U U21   6
Other University Matches
OU Greyhounds	41	CU LX Club	15
CU U21A	16	OU Whippets	19
Cambridge U Colls	3	Oxford U Colls	29

Women's University Match
Oxford U   35   Cambridge U   7
Women's University Second Teams Match
Cambridge U   12   Oxford U   0

British Universities Sports Association
Men's Winners: Loughborough University
Women's Winners: UWIC

Inter-Services Champions: The Army
Hospitals Cup Winners: Imperial Medicals

Middlesex Sevens
Winners: Gloucester
Runners-up: Wasps

Rosslyn Park Schools Sevens
Festival Winners: Colston's
Colts Winners: Epsom College
Junior Winners: Brynteg School
Preparatory Schools Winners: Bedford School
Girls Schools Winners: Colston's
Open Winners: Millfield School

Daily Mail Schools Day
Under 18 Cup Winners: St Peter's Gloucester
Under 18 Vase Winners: Lymm High School
Under 15 Cup Winners: Bedford School
Under 15 Vase Winners: Langley Park BS

RFUW Rugby World National Cup: Saracens
Women's Champions: Richmond
Women's Sevens Champions: Richmond

'Fan'atical

An unbridled passion
for the game

Positive Energy

SCOTLAND

BT Cup Final
Currie	15	Watsonians	31

BT Shield Final
Ellon	14	West of Scotland	20

BT Bowl Final
Morgan Academy FP	39	Highland	19

Scottish Sevens Winners
Kelso: Selkirk
Selkirk: Royal Scots
Gala: Boroughmuir
Melrose: Newcastle Falcons
Hawick: Newcastle Falcons
Berwick: Jed-Forest
Langholm: Newcastle Falcons
Peebles: Boroughmuir
Earlston: Jed-Forest
Jed-Forest: Heriot's
Kings of Sevens: Jed-Forest

BT Scotland Premiership
Division One

	P	W	D	L	F	A	BP	Pts
Glasgow Hawks	22	18	1	3	643	349	16	90
Watsonians	22	17	1	4	535	381	10	80
Aberdeen GSFP	22	12	1	9	554	466	15	65
Currie	22	9	1	12	495	418	15	53
Hawick	22	12	0	10	388	429	5	53
Melrose	22	11	0	11	487	535	9	53
Ayr	22	10	1	11	530	533	9	51
Heriot's RC	22	9	0	13	549	570	15	51
Boroughmuir	22	9	1	12	505	541	4	50
Stewart's Melville	22	11	0	11	422	545	4	48
Biggar	22	7	0	15	423	584	7	35
Stirling County	22	4	0	18	384	570	9	25

Champions: Glasgow Hawks
Relegated: Stewart's Melville FP, Biggar and Stirling County
Note: For the 2006-07 season there will only be ten clubs in Division One

Division Two

	P	W	D	L	F	A	BP	Pts
Dundee HSFP	22	18	0	4	794	305	18	90
Cartha QP	22	17	0	5	625	281	15	83
Edinburgh Acads	22	16	0	6	563	419	11	75
Jed-Forest	22	13	1	8	458	417	7	61
Selkirk	22	11	2	9	498	409	11	59
Gala	22	10	0	12	341	461	7	47
Kelso	22	9	3	10	380	427	4	46
Hillhead/J'hill	22	10	0	12	398	566	5	45
GHA	22	8	1	13	479	523	10	44
Berwick	22	7	2	13	322	471	5	37
Haddington	22	6	1	15	340	488	7	21
M'field Wdrs	22	2	0	20	269	698	4	12

Champions: Dundee HSFP
Relegated: Murrayfield Wanderers
Promoted from Division Three: Hamilton
Note: For the 2006-07 season Divisions Two and Three will each consist of 12 clubs

WALES

Konica Minolta Cup
Quarter-finals
Cardiff	10	Llandovery	0
Maesteg	27	Newport	8
Pontypridd	28	Builth Wells	15
Swansea	13	Neath	33

Semi-finals
Maesteg	9	Neath	50
Cardiff	13	Pontypridd	23

Final
Neath	25	Pontypridd	26

Welsh Premiership

	P	W	D	L	F	A	Pts	Tries
Neath	30	28	0	2	1070	421	84	141
Bridgend	30	23	0	7	709	587	69	81
Pontypridd	30	21	0	9	788	560	63	93
Aberavon	30	19	0	11	748	596	57	81
Newport	30	19	0	11	623	610	57	58
Llanelli	30	18	0	12	589	599	54	68
Swansea	30	16	0	14	849	713	48	102
Bedwas	30	12	2	16	562	702	38	52
Cross Keys	30	12	0	18	513	608	33	73
Cardiff	30	11	0	19	646	726	33	73
Glamorgan Wdrs	30	10	2	18	607	738	32	71
Ebbw Vale	30	10	1	19	583	686	31	66
Llandovery	30	10	0	20	597	692	30	58
Maesteg	30	9	1	20	573	785	28	64
Carmarthen Q	30	9	1	20	573	785	52	28
Pontypool	30	8	3	19	473	632	27	53

Relegated: Carmarthen Quins and Pontypool

Welsh Leagues
Division One

	P	W	D	L	F	A	Pts
Bonymaen	30	25	2	3	1034	382	77
Whitland	30	22	2	6	773	329	68
Beddau	30	22	0	8	841	424	66
Newbridge	30	20	1	9	633	514	61
Merthyr	30	20	0	10	821	608	60
Cwmllynfell	30	18	2	10	753	532	56
Blackwood	30	17	3	10	696	563	54
Llangennech	30	14	0	16	702	633	42
Caerphilly	30	13	0	17	576	810	39
Llanharan	29	12	0	17	606	680	36
UWIC	30	11	1	18	724	912	34
Builth Wells	29	11	0	18	554	685	33
Narberth	30	9	0	21	465	762	27
Waunarlwydd	30	8	1	21	395	829	22
Fleur de Lys	30	7	0	23	417	861	21
Ystrad Rhondda	30	3	2	25	350	816	8*

* Indicates three points deducted

Promoted from Divisions 2 East and West respectively: Bargoed, Newport Saracens, Abercynon; Dunvant, Bridgend Athletic, Loughor
Note: For the 2006-07 season Division One has been reconfigured as two divisions (East and West) of 12 clubs each

IRELAND

AIB League
Division One

	P	W	D	L	F	A	BP	Pts
Garryowen	15	14	0	1	379	180	5	61
Clontarf	15	12	0	3	403	222	13	61
Cork Const	15	12	0	3	384	216	8	56
Shannon	15	13	0	2	357	200	4	56
UL Bohemians	15	10	1	4	345	309	7	49
Belfast H'quins	15	8	0	7	328	330	7	39
Buccaneers	15	7	1	7	305	261	7	37
Lansdowne	15	7	0	8	337	311	4	32
UC Dublin	15	6	0	9	295	286	8	32
Ballymena	15	7	0	8	307	313	4	32
St Mary's College	15	6	1	8	250	305	3	29
Dungannon	15	6	0	9	264	357	5	29
Blackrock College	15	4	1	10	213	376	5	23
Galwegians	15	3	0	12	208	343	7	19
Dublin University	15	3	0	12	265	399	5	17
County Carlow	15	0	0	15	191	479	5	5

Relegated to Division Two: Dublin University and County Carlow

AIB League Play-offs
Semi-finals

Garryowen	20	Shannon	21
Clontarf	26	Cork Constitution	6

Final

Shannon	30	Clontarf	3

Division Two
Champions: Terenure College
Runners-up: Dolphin (promoted)

Division Three
Champions: Clonakilty
Runners-up: Suttonians

Senior Cup Winners
Munster: Shannon
Leinster: Clontarf
Ulster: Belfast Harlequins
Connacht: Buccaneers

Senior League Winners
Munster: UL Bohemians
Leinster: Monkstown
Ulster: Ballymena and Dungannon
Connacht: Buccaneers

CELTIC LEAGUE

	P	W	D	L	F	A	BP	Pts
Ulster	20	15	1	4	510	347	5	75
Leinster	20	14	0	6	545	427	10	74
Munster	20	12	0	8	439	372	10	66
Blues	20	11	0	9	418	415	8	63
Edinburgh	20	11	0	9	418	415	8	60
Ospreys	20	11	0	9	381	409	3	55
Scarlets	20	10	1	9	418	402	7	53
Dragons	20	7	0	13	355	456	9	45
Borders	20	7	0	13	386	501	9	44
Glasgow	20	5	0	15	371	439	9	37
Connacht	20	6	0	14	325	466	5	37

Note: The reason for the apparent discrepancy in points accrued is that for each free weekend four points were awarded to the clubs concerned

FRANCE

'Top 14' Play-offs

Semi-finals

Stade Toulousain	12	Stade Francais	9
Biarritz	12	Perpignan	9

Final

Biarritz	40	Stade Toulousain	13

ITALY

'Super 10'

Final

Benetton Treviso	17	Calvisano	12

NEW ZEALAND

National Provincial Championship 2005

Final

Auckland	39	Otago	11

Ranfurly Shield holders: Canterbury

SOUTH AFRICA

Currie Cup 2005

Final

Cheetahs	29	Blue Bulls	25

BARBARIANS

Opponents	Results
Combined Services	W 45-6
East Midlands	W 63-17
Leicester	W 52-42
Royal Navy	W 31-10
ENGLAND	L 19-46
SCOTLAND	L 19-66
GEORGIA	W 28-11

Played 7 Won 5 Lost 2

SUPER 14 TOURNAMENT 2006

Semi-finals

Hurricanes	16	Waratahs	14
Crusaders	35	Bulls	15

Final

Crusaders	19	Hurricanes	12

HEINEKEN CUP 2006

Quarter-finals

Leicester	12	Bath	15
Toulouse	35	Leinster	41
Munster	19	Perpignan	10
Biarritz	11	Sale	6

Semi-finals

Biarritz	18	Bath	9
Leinster	6	Munster	30

Final

Biarritz	19	Munster	23

EUROPEAN CHALLENGE CUP 2006

Quarter-finals

Newcastle	23	Connacht	3
Gloucester	46	Brive	13
Northampton	25	Worcester	34
London Irish	48	Bayonne	5

Semi-finals

Gloucester	31	Worcester	23
Newcastle	22	London Irish	27

Final

Gloucester	36	London Irish	34

All the materials to tackle any situation

PREVIEW OF THE
SEASON 2006-07

Key Players 2006-07

by IAN ROBERTSON

ENGLAND

MATHEW TAIT

An 18-year-old Tait was signed to Newcastle in 2004 and made his debut for the club in a Zurich Premiership game against London Irish, in which he scored a try with his first touch of the ball. However, he had a harsh introduction to international rugby against Wales in 2005, in which match he was the victim of a number of big tackles from Gavin Henson before eventually being replaced. Andy Robinson then dropped him from the national side. Since this rather rude awakening, Tait has been showing a growing maturity with Newcastle and electric pace and strength and excellent cover defence with England's sevens squad – he was top try scorer at the 2006 Commonwealth Games in Melbourne. Such was his performance that he was brought back into the full England squad, playing in both of the 2006 summer Tests against Australia, where unfortunately England did not enjoy much success. However, Mathew Tait is definitely ready to retake a more permanent place in the England set-up. If anybody is going to give the side a new vision behind the scrum it is the young Newcastle centre.

LEWIS MOODY

The Leicester flanker made his England debut in Canada in 2001 and was a member of the 2005 Lions touring squad. Since his first appearance, Moody has proved to be utterly fearless and tremendously consistent. When fit, the 28-year-old is the automatic choice for the number 7 shirt for both club and country. Even in England's darkest moments he continues to run around, epitomising work rate and enthusiasm. However, he has a fiery temper, which led him to be the first player to be sent off in a Test match at Twickenham with his dismissal for punching against Samoa last season. He also has a tendency to give away too many penalties, but that is maybe because England have struggled to put any patterns together and as a result his negative side has always been highlighted rather than his compelling positive. His hands are as good as his tackling, and he won the final line out in the phase of play that led to Jonny Wilkinson's dropped goal in the 2003 World Cup final. If England do ever find their rhythm, Lewis Moody will be able to show what a constructive player he can be.

SCOTLAND

MIKE BLAIR

Blair's international debut came in 2002 against Canada, and he marked the occasion by scoring a try. Over the past couple of seasons he has been locked in a fierce battle for the Scotland number 9 shirt with Lions scrum half Chris Cusiter. This rivalry seems to have benefited his game greatly and he is now first choice for the national side. He has acted as vice-captain for Scotland and has been cited as one of the team's most promising players and consistently gives world-class displays.

JASON WHITE

White could once have been described as somewhat of a bit-part player, but since being appointed national captain the Sale flanker has become Scotland's stand-out forward and arguably one of the most physical back-rowers in the game. He has an incredible work rate and is massive in defence. He is a fantastic smash-tackler and renowned as being one of the hardest hitters in the northern hemisphere. The back-rower led Scotland in their famous win against France in 2006 at Murrayfield, in which match he also earned his fiftieth cap. Shortly after, he led his national side to another victory at Murrayfield, this time over England, thereby recovering the Calcutta Cup. He received the Man of the Match award for his outstanding contribution to the win. White has been recognised numerous other times for his talent and achievements; his accolades include the Scottish PRA Player of the Year and the PFA Player of the Year awards for 2006.

WALES

DWAYNE PEEL

Peel came through the Llanelli finishing school of scrum halves and is now the Scarlets' most influential first choice. The scrum half made his Wales senior debut as a replacement against Japan in 2001. A few seasons ago he was locked in three-way combat with Gareth Cooper and Mike Phillips for the Welsh number 9 shirt, but Peel has since broken away from the rest with his accurate service, speed on the break and, above all, shrewd assessment of what is happening. As a result, the scrum-half shirt for Wales and for the Lions became his, and since the autumn series of 2004 he has become a regular starter for the national side. Peel had an impressive 2005 Six Nations tournament, winning two Man of the Match awards as Wales stormed to the Grand Slam. He then fulfilled his dream of becoming a British Lion on the 2005 summer tour to New Zealand, appearing in all three Test matches against the All Blacks. However, an injury to his shoulder sustained during the Six Nations match against Italy kept him out of the rest of the tournament. Although he was sorely missed by Wales, he was painfully aware of Mike Phillips taking full advantage, standing out against France. Still, competition will surely bring out the very best in the 25-year-old Peel.

RYAN JONES

The Ospreys flanker has barely played for a full year after having a season out following reconstructive surgery on his shoulder. However, the back-row forward left such a huge mark on the international stage that all he has to do is burst onto the scene in the same manner as he first did in the Welsh Grand Slam season of 2005. He began that season as a stand-in for Dafydd Jones against South Africa and ended it as first-choice Lions back-rower in New Zealand. He is a hugely physical player and has a fantastic work rate all around the park, especially on the floor, frustrating opponents by stealing the ball. Clive Woodwood was so impressed with Jones's impact on the international scene that he flew the flanker out to New Zealand following Simon Taylor's hamstring injury. He played so well in a 30-19 win over Otago that he was called into the squad for the first Test. He came on as a replacement and went on to start in the final two Tests and was considered by many to be one of the stars of the tour. While he has been away he has bulked up without sacrificing any of his explosive pace, and is currently taking part in pre-season training with the Ospreys, preparing for a potentially fantastic year.

IRELAND

SHANE HORGAN

Over the past couple of seasons, the Leinster man has struggled to find his true position for both club and country. However, in last season's Six Nations he appeared to have settled out on the wing, with excellent results as a devastating finisher. Horgan was also one of the few outstanding successes of the 2005 Lions tour. Standing at 6ft 4ins and weighing over 15 stones, he is a hugely imposing and powerful winger, but his strength is his prime attribute both when on the ball and in defensive positions. Horgan also has the versatility and speed that are so valuable in the modern game. However, his physical approach has meant that since he marked his international debut against Scotland in 2000 with a try, he has had more than his fair share of injuries. He has won many admirers as his injuries are seen as testament to a real commitment to the game and a willingness to put his body on the line for the cause. He also achieved national hero status in 2006 when he scored the winning try against England at Twickenham to secure Ireland the Triple Crown for the second time in three years.

DONNCHA O'CALLAGHAN

O'Callaghan has made huge progress since he finally secured a starting spot as an Ireland lock in last season's Six Nations. Previously, since his debut against Wales in 2003, his international career had been as a replacement, coming onto the pitch for Malcolm O'Kelly. However, for Munster and on the 2005 Lions tour to New Zealand, O'Callaghan became a force of nature in his own right. He is a tremendously physical player with good hands. He gets around the pitch at a fair pace and is not afraid to put his head among the boots. He can have hot flushes at times, but he is graceful in the air and has a high work rate.

FRANCE

YANNICK JAUZION

The Toulouse centre made his debut against South Africa in 2001 and has since made a huge impact on world rugby. He was justifiably named best player and best international at the French Rugby Awards in 2005. Powerful in attack and strong defensively, Jauzion is pure French class, full of subtlety and grace, his running complemented by a big right boot when needs be. He has a tremendous ability to offload in the tackle, breaking the gain line and allowing support to receive the ball at speed. He is tall, fast, strong and intelligent, and is a good crash player, a combination which makes him arguably the best centre in the world. He missed most of the 2006 Six Nations with a toe injury, and without him France were never totally fluent. In fact it is fair to say that France, desperate to win the World Cup in 2007 on home soil, will be carefully monitoring every bone in their centre's body.

JEROME THION

Thion is not yet as visible as his venerable, conspicuous second-row partner Fabien Pelous, who has dominated French second-row play for the past decade. However, Thion of Biarritz is a youthful workhorse and an integral part of the formidable backbone of the French scrum. He made his Test debut for France on the 2003 tour to Argentina and New Zealand and has since established himself as a potential long-term successor to Pelous after captaining the side during the three autumn Tests in late 2005, all of which France won. Thion has a powerful presence at mauls and in the scrum, and has good handling ability. He is gradually earning himself a solid reputation and is growing in confidence with the ball in hand.

ITALY

PAUL GRIFFEN

The Kiwi-turned-Azzurro made his debut for Italy in 2004 against England in the Six Nations and proved to be hugely influential in the tournament. He was voted Italy's best player alongside Andrea Lo Cicero. The Calvisano scrum half has a phenomenal work rate and is utterly fearless in defence. He plays with real spirit and is inventive with a good eye for the opposition's defence. He came into replace Italy's most experienced player ever, Alessandro Troncon, so it was never going to be easy for him, but already the New Zealander has reached icon status.

SERGIO PARISSE

Parisse was born 23 years ago in La Plata in Argentina, but Italian rugby was in his blood. His father, Sergio Parisse senior, won the Italian championship with L'Aquila in the 1960s and 1970s. There is a further Continental ingredient in the No. 8's make-up as he plays his club rugby for Stade Francais in Paris. Parisse was discovered by the Italian Under 19 squad bound for the World Cup in Chile and made his debut for the full Italian side in New Zealand in 2002. He quickly established himself as one of Italy's key players and is a natural ball-carrying No. 8. He is very strong and direct and loves contact but has soft hands when required. He does have a tendency to get injured – he sustained a serious thigh injury in 2004 – but when fit is an extremely bright prospect.

Fixtures 2006-07

AUGUST 2006
Sat, 26th   Scottish Premiership 1–3 (1)
            Scottish Nat Lges 1-3 (1)

SEPTEMBER 2006
Fri, 1st to
Sun, 3rd   Celtic League
Sat, 2nd   National Leagues 1-3 (1)
            Welsh Premier League (1)
            Scottish Premiership 1-3 (2)
            Scottish Nat Lges 1-3 (2)

Sat, 2nd to
Sun, 3rd   English Premiership (1)
Fri, 8th to
Sun, 10th   English Premiership (2)
            Celtic League
Sat, 9th   National Leagues 1-3 (2)
            National Leagues (12s) (1)
            Welsh Konica Minolta Cup Rd 1
            Welsh Premier League (2)
            Scottish Premiership 1-3 (3)
            Scottish Nat Lges 1-3 (3)

Tue, 12th to
Wed, 13th   Celtic League
Fri, 15th to
Sun, 17th   English Premiership (3)
            Celtic League
Sat, 16th   National Leagues 1-3 (3)
            National Leagues (12s) (2)
            Junior Vase Preliminary Round
            Welsh Premier League (3)
            Scottish Premiership 1-3 (4)
            Scottish Nat Lges 1-3 (4)

Fri, 22nd to
Sun, 24th   English Premiership (4)
            Celtic League
Sat, 23rd   National Leagues 1-3 (4)
            National Leagues (12s) (3)
            National Leagues (10s) (1)
            Welsh Premier League (4)
            Scottish Premiership 1-3 (5)
            Scottish Nat Lges 1-3 (5)

Fri, 29th to
Sun, 1st Oct   Celtic League
Sat, 30th   National Leagues 1-3 (5)
            National Leagues (12s) (4)
            National Leagues (10s) (2)
            Welsh Konica Minolta Cup Rd 2
            Welsh Premier League (5)
            Scottish Premiership 1-3 (6)
            Scottish Nat Lges 1-3 (6)

OCTOBER 2006
Fri, 6th to
Sun, 8th   Celtic League
Sat, 7th   National Leagues 1-3 (6)
            National Leagues (12s) (5)

            Junior Vase First Round
            Welsh Premier League (6)
            Scottish Premiership 1-3 (7)
            Scottish Nat Lges 1-3 (7)

Fri, 13th to
Sun, 15th   English Premiership (5)
            Celtic League
Sat, 14th   National Leagues 1-3 (7)
            National Leagues (12s) (6)
            National Leagues (10s) (3)
            Welsh Premier League (7)
            Scottish Premiership 1-3 (8)
            Scottish Nat Lges 1-3 (8)
            AIB Irish Leagues (1)

Fri, 20th to
Sun, 22nd   European Cups Round One
Sat, 21st   National Leagues 1-3 (8)
            National Leagues (12s) (7)
            National Leagues (10s) (4)
            Welsh Konica Minolta Cup Rd 3
            Welsh Premier League (8)
            Scottish Premiership 1-3 (9)
            Scottish Nat Lges 1-3 (9)
            AIB Irish Leagues (2)

Fri, 27th to
Sun, 29th   European Cups Round Two
Sat, 28th   National Leagues 1 & 2 (9)
            National Trophy First Round
            Intermediate Cup First Round
            Junior Vase Second Round
            Welsh Premier League (9)
            Scottish Premiership 1-3 (10)
            Scottish Nat Lges 1-3 (10)
            AIB Irish Leagues (3)

NOVEMBER 2006
Fri, 3rd to
Sat, 4th   English Premiership (6)
Fri, 3rd to
Sun, 5th   Celtic League
Sat, 4th   ENGLAND v NEW ZEALAND
                (Twickenham)
            WALES v AUSTRALIA
                (Cardiff)
            National Leagues 1 & 2 (10)
            National League 3 (9)
            National Leagues (12s) (8)
            National Leagues (10s) (5)
            Scottish Premiership 1-3 (11)
            Scottish Nat Lges 1-3 (11)
            AIB Irish Leagues (4)
Fri, 10th   Welsh Premier League (10)
Fri, 10th to
Sun, 12th   English Premiership (7)
            Celtic League
Sat, 11th   ENGLAND v ARGENTINA
                (Twickenham)

SCOTLAND v ROMANIA
(Murrayfield)
WALES v PACIFIC ISLANDS
(Cardiff)
National Leagues 1 & 2 (11)
National League 3 (10)
National Leagues (12s) (9)
National Leagues (10s) (6)
Scottsh Premiership 1-3 (12)
Scottish Nat Lges 1-3 (12)

Fri, 17th   WALES v CANADA
(Cardiff)
Fri, 17th to
Sat, 18th   English Premiership (8)
Fri, 17th to
Sun, 19th   Celtic League
Sat 18th   ENGLAND v SOUTH AFRICA
(Twickenham)
SCOTLAND v PACIFIC ISLANDS
(Murrayfield)
National League 1 (12)
National Trophy Second Round
Intermediate Cup Second Rd
Junior Vase Third Round
Welsh Premier League (11)
Scottish Premiership 1-3 (13)
Scottish Nat Lges 1-3 (13)

Fri, 24th to
Sun, 26th   English Premiership (9)
Celtic League
Sat, 25th   ENGLAND v SOUTH AFRICA
(Twickenham)
SCOTLAND v AUSTRALIA
(Murrayfield)
WALES v NEW ZEALAND
(Cardiff)
National League 1 (13)
National League 2 (12)
National League 3 (11)
National Leagues (12s) (10)
National Leagues (10s) (7)

DECEMBER 2006

Fri, 1st to
Sun, 3rd   Celtic League
AIB Irish Leagues (5)
Sat, 2nd   National League 1 (14)
National League 2 (13)
National League 3 (12)
National Leagues (12s) (11)
National Leagues (10s) (8)
Welsh Premier League (12)
Scottish Premiership 1-3 (14)
Scottish Nat Lges 1-3 (14)

Fri, 8th to
Sun, 10th   European Cups Round Three
Sat, 9th   National League 1 (15)
National Trophy Third Round
Intermediate Cup Third Round
Junior Vase Fourth Round
Welsh Premier League (13)

Scottish Premiership 1-3 (15)
Scottish Cup First Round
AIB Irish Leagues (6)
Tue, 12th   OXFORD v CAMBRIDGE
(Twickenham)
Fri, 15th to
Sun, 17th   European Cups Round Four
AIB Irish Leagues (7)
Sat, 16th   National League 1 (16)
National League 2 (14)
National League 3 (13)
National Leagues (12s) (12)
National Leagues (10s) (9)
Welsh Konica Minolta Cup Rd 4
Welsh Premier League (14)
Scottish Premiership 1-3 (16)
Scottish Nat Lges 1-3 (15)
Fri, 22nd   English Premiership (10)
Fri, 22nd to
Sun, 24th   Celtic League
Sat, 23rd   National League 1 (17)
National League 2 (15)
National League 3 (14)
Scottish Premiership 1-3 (17)
Tue, 26th   Welsh Premier League (15)
Tue, 26th to
Wed, 27th   English Premiership (11)
Tue, 26th to
Thu, 28th   Celtic League
Fri, 29th to
Sun, 31st   Celtic League
Sat, 30th   National League 1 (18)
Welsh Premier League (16)

JANUARY 2007

Mon, 1st   English Premiership (12)
Fri, 5th to
Sun, 7th   Celtic League
Sat, 6th   National League 1 (19)
National League 2 (16)
National League 3 (15)
National Leagues (12s) (13)
National Leagues (10s) (10)
Welsh Premier League (17)
Scottish Nat Lges 1-3 (16)
P1 Super Cup (1) Scotland
AIB Irish Leagues (8)

Sat, 6th to
Sun, 7th   English Premiership (13)
Fri, 12th to
Sun, 14th   European Cups Round Five
Sat, 13th   National League 1 (20)
National League 2 (17)
National League 3 (16)
National Leagues (12s) (14)
National Leagues (10s) (11)
Welsh Premier League (18)
Scottish Premiership 1-3 (18)
Scottish Nat Lges 1-3 (17)
Fri, 19th to
Sun, 21st   European Cups Round Six

Sat, 20th	AIB Irish Leagues (9)
	National Trophy Fourth Round
	Intermediate Cup Fourth Rd
	Junior Vase Fifth Round
	Scottish Cup Second Round
Fri, 26th to	
Sun, 28th	English Premiership (14)
	Celtic League
Sat, 27th	National League 1 (21)
	National League 2 (18)
	National League 3 (17)
	National Leagues (12s) (15)
	National Leagues (10s) (12)
	Welsh Konica Minolta Cup Rd 5
	Welsh Premier League (19)
	Scottish Premiership 2, 3 (19)
	Scottish Nat Lges 1-3 (18)
	P1 Super Cup (2) Scotland
	AIB Irish Leagues (10)

FEBRUARY 2007

Fri, 2nd	England v Scotland (U 21s)
	Italy v France (Under 21s)
Sat, 3rd	ENGLAND v SCOTLAND
	(Twickenham)
	ITALY v FRANCE (Rome)
	Wales v Ireland (Under 21s)
	National League 1 (22)
	National League 2 (19)
	National League 3 (18)
	National Leagues (12s) (16)
	Welsh Premier League (20)
	Scottish Cup Third Round
Sun, 4th	WALES v IRELAND (Cardiff)
Fri, 9th	Scotland v Wales (Under 21s)
Sat, 10th	ENGLAND v ITALY
	(Twickenham)
	SCOTLAND v WALES
	(Murrayfield)
	National Trophy Fifth Round
	Intermediate Cup Fifth Round
	Junior Vase Sixth Round
Fri, 16th to	
Sun, 18th	Celtic League
Sat, 17th	National League 1 (23)
	National League 2 (20)
	National League 3 (19)
	National Leagues (12s) (17)
	National Leagues (10s) (13)
	Welsh Konica Minolta Cup Rd 6
	Scottish Premiership 2, 3 (20)
	Scottish Nat Lges 1-3 (19)
	P1 Super Cup (3) Scotland
	AIB Irish Leagues (11)
Sat, 17th to	
Sun, 18th	English Premiership (15)
Fri, 23rd	Ireland v England (Under 21s)
	Scotland v Italy (Under 21s)
	France v Wales (Under 21s)
Fri, 23rd to	
Sat, 24th	English Premiership (16)

Sat, 24th	IRELAND v ENGLAND (Dublin)
	SCOTLAND v ITALY
	(Murrayfield)
	FRANCE v WALES (Paris)
	National League 1 (24)
	National League 2 (21)
	National League 3 (20)
	National Leagues (12s) (18)
	National Leagues (10s) (14)

MARCH 2007

Fri 2nd to	
Sun, 4th	Celtic League
Sat, 3rd	National League 3 (21)
	National Leagues (12s) (19)
	National Leagues (10s) (15)
	National Trophy Quarter-Finals
	Intermediate Cup Q-Finals
	Junior Vase Quarter-Finals
	Welsh Premier League (21)
	Scottish Premiership 2, 3 (21)
	Scottish Nat Lges 1-3 (20)
	P1 Super Cup (4) Scotland
	AIB Irish Leagues (12)
Sat, 3rd to	
Sun, 4th	English Premiership (17)
Fri, 9th	England v France (Under 21s)
	Scotland v Ireland (Under 21s)
	Italy v Wales (Under 21s)
Fri, 9th to	
Sat, 10th	English Premiership (18)
Sat, 10th	ENGLAND v FRANCE
	(Twickenham)
	SCOTLAND v IRELAND
	(Murrayfield)
	ITALY v WALES (Rome)
	National League 1 (25)
Fri, 16th	Wales v England (Under 21s)
	France v Scotland (Under 21s)
	Welsh Premier League (22)
Fri, 16th to	
Sun, 18th	English Premiership (19)
Sat, 17th	WALES v ENGLAND (Cardiff)
	FRANCE v SCOTLAND (Paris)
	National League 1 (26)
	National Leagues 2 & 3 (22)
	National Leagues (12s) (20)
	National Leagues (10s) (16)
	Scottish Cup Fourth Round
Fri, 23rd to	
Sun, 25th	Celtic League
Sat, 24th	National League 3 (23)
	National Trophy Semi-Finals
	Intermediate Cup Semi-Finals
	Junior Vase Semi-Finals
	Welsh Konica Minolta Cup Q-Fs
	Welsh Premier League (23)
	Scottish Premiership 2, 3 (22)
	Scottish Nat Lges 1-3 (21)
	P1 Super Cup (5) Scotland
	AIB Irish Leagues (13)

Fri, 30th to
Sun, 1st Apr   European Cups Quarter-Finals
Sat, 31st   National League 1 (27)
National League 2 (23)
National League 3 (24)
National Leagues (12s) (21)
National Leagues (10s) (17)
National Under 20
        Championship Q-Finals
Welsh Premier League (24)
Scottish Nat Lges 1-3 (22)
P1 Super Cup Final Scotland

APRIL 2007
Fri, 6th to
Sun, 8th   English Premiership (20)
Celtic League
Sat, 7th   National League 1 (28)
Welsh Premier League (25)
Scottish Cup Quarter-Finals
AIB Irish Leagues (14)

Fri, 13th to
Sun, 15th   English Premiership (21)
Celtic League
Sat, 14th   National Trophy Final
        (Twickenham)
Intermediate Cup and Junior
        Vase Finals
        (Twickenham)
National League 2 (24)
National League 3 (25)
National Leagues (12s) (22)
National Leagues (10s) (18)
Welsh Konica Minolta Cup S-Fs
Welsh Premier League (26)

Tue, 17th to
Thu, 19th   Celtic League
Fri, 20th to
Sun, 22nd   European Cups Semi-Finals
Sat, 21st   National League 1 (29)
National League 2 (25)
National League 3 (26)
Scottish Cup Semi-Finals
AIB Irish Leagues (15)

Fri, 27th to
Sun, 29th   Celtic League

Sat, 28th   English Premiership (22)
National League 1 (30)
National League 2 (26)
National Leagues 3, 12s &
        10s Play-Offs
County Championship Plate Rd 1
National Under 20
        Championship S-Finals

MAY 2007
Fri, 4th to
Sun, 6th   Celtic League
Sat, 5th   Royal Navy v Army
        (Twickenham)
Welsh Konica Minolta Cup Final
Scottish Cup Finals Day
        (Murrayfield)
County Championship Rd 1
County Championship Plate Rd 2
Sat, 5th to
Sun, 6th   English Premiership Semi-Finals
Fri, 11th to
Sun, 13th   Celtic League
Sat, 12th   County Championship Rd 2
County Championship Plate Rd 3
Sat, 12th or
Sun, 13th   English Premiership Final
        (Twickenham)
Fri, 18th/
Sun, 20th   European Challenge Cup Final
Sat, 19th
or Sun, 20th   Heineken Cup Final
        (Twickenham)
County Championship Rd 3
County Championship Plate S-Fs
Sat, 26th   ENGLAND INTERNATIONAL
        (to be confirmed)
County Championship
        and Plate Finals
        (Twickenham)
National Under 20
        Championship Final
        (Twickenham)

Wooden Spoon

Mission Statement

Wooden Spoon aims to enhance the quality and
prospect of life for children and young persons in the
United Kingdom who are presently disadvantaged either
physically, mentally or socially

Charity Registration No: 326691

THE SPORTING CLUB

PROUD SUPPORTERS OF WOODEN SPOON

"GOOD FOOD IN A RELAXING ATMOSPHERE, WITH SUPERB AFTER DINNER SPEAKERS"

Now in its sixteenth year, the Sporting Club successfully administrates Clubs in nine areas of the Midlands, West Country and London. The principal objective of Sporting Club Dinners is to provide members with the environment in which to entertain clients, colleagues or friends in pleasant surroundings with excellent speakers from the World of Sport.

The Clubs	Venues
Capital	The London Marriott, Grosvenor Square and The Brewery Chiswell Street
East Midlands	East Midlands Conference Centre
Gloucestershire	Thistle Hotel, Cheltenham
North Worcestershire	Worcester Rugby Club
Solihull	The Renaissance Hotel, Solihull
South Staffordshire	The Molineux, Wolverhampton F C
South Warwickshire	Warwick Hilton, Warwick
Sutton Coldfield	Ramada Hotel, Sutton Coldfield
West Country	Marriott Hotel, Bristol

Previous speakers have included:-

Sports	Sporting Speakers
Rugby	Jason Leonard OBE, Gareth Edwards, Will Carling OBE
Cricket	Shane Warne, Dickie Bird MBE, Ian Botham OBE
Snooker	Steve Davis OBE, John Parrott MBE, Denis Taylor
Football	Sir Geoff Hurst, Jack Charlton OBE, Jimmy Greaves
Boxing	Sir Henry Cooper, Alan Minter, John H Stracey
Others	Sir Stirling Moss, Sir Ranulph Fiennes, Roger Black MBE

If you wish to attend a Sporting Club Dinner please contact
David Trick
Telephone: 01373 830720   Facsimile: 01373 830999
Email - david@sportingclubgroup.com

Or Visit www.sportingclubgroup.com for further details

The Sporting Club (UK) Ltd, P O Box 3582, Laverton, Bath, BA2 7ZR